TO BEND
WITHOUT
BREAKING

TO BEND WITHOUT BREAKING

Mary Ella Stuart

ABINGDON
Nashville

TO BEND WITHOUT BREAKING

Copyright © 1977 by Abingdon

Library of Congress Cataloging in Publication Data

Stuart, Mary Ella, 1909-
To bend without breaking.
1. Stress (Psychology) 2. Conduct of life.
I. Title
BF575.S75S78   158'.1   77-6797

ISBN 0-687-42160-8

Scripture is from The New Testament in Modern English, copyright © J. B. Phillips 1958, 1960, 1972.

The Twelve Steps are from Alcoholics Anonymous, copyright © 1939, by Alcoholics Anonymous World Services, Inc. Reprinted by permission of Alcoholics Anonymous World Services, Inc.

Text on p. 89 is from the article "Worship" by Charles McCabe (*San Francisco Chronicle*, December 9, 1975). © Chronicle Publishing Co., 1975.

Text on p. 85 is from p. 112 in LIFE TOGETHER by Dietrich Bonhoeffer, Harper & Row, 1954.

Text on pp. 48-49 is from pp. 129-30 in THE HEART OF MAN by Erich Fromm. Volume Twelve of Religious Perspectives, planned and edited by Ruth Nanda Anshen, Harper & Row, 1964.

Text on pp. 38 and 85 is from p. 331 and abridged and adapted from p. 126 in CAPTAIN NEWMAN, M.D. by Leo Rosten. Copyright © 1961 by Leo Rosten.

Text on pp. 32-33 is from HOW TO BE YOUR OWN BEST FRIEND, by Mildred Newman and Bernard Berkowitz, © 1973 by Random House, Inc.

Text on p. 107 is from "New Year's Eve," COLLECTED POEMS OF C. DAY-LEWIS. Used by permission of the publishers, Jonathan Cape Ltd. and Hogarth Press, and the executors of the C. Day-Lewis estate.

MANUFACTURED BY THE PARTHENON PRESS AT NASHVILLE, TENNESSEE, UNITED STATES OF AMERICA

To my husband and my son
who have shared with me
both the agony and the
ecstasy of this story

Acknowledgments

There is no way possible I may acknowledge the many persons and groups of persons who have been of help and from whom I have learned some of the techniques of dealing with stress. I wish to specifically say thank you to those of you who have directly had some influence upon the writing of this book.

To my son Rob for believing all the way along that I could, in fact, write a book and for encouraging me to do so. His editing and helping the manuscript take shape and form has been invaluable.

To Helen Flegal, a dear friend for many years and a counselor, who kept insisting that I must put my ideas down in a book and who suggested the title.

To Dr. Evelyn Miller Berger, my longtime counselor friend whose spiritual experience and psychological insight guided me during the trying years when I sought to recover my health.

To our dear friends Tom and Betty Carpenter who have shared many concepts of Alcoholics Anonymous and Alanon as well as those of the National Council on Alcoholism, of which Tom served as president.

To Muriel Byram, my friend of thirty-five years who contributed the mantra and who was responsible along with the Reverend Don Kuhn for instituting my first stress class. She has been a sounding board and critic for many of the key ideas and viewpoints expressed herein, as well as a source of great personal inspiration and comfort.

To Laura Kruse, my husband's present secretary, and Beth Fogg, his first secretary, for endless hours of patient and skilled typing, copying, and assisting with editing.

To members of my beloved Anx Anon who allowed me to share their thinking at a time when we were all suffering a great deal of stress and for their continued support and friendship over the years.

To Dr. Joseph D. Chadwick, Fellow of Stanford Research Institute in Menlo Park, California, for sharing with me a copy of the Holmes and Rahe Social Readjustment Rating Scale from which the stress chart in Appendix B is taken. And to Dr. Holmes himself for allowing its frequent adaptation and use.

To members of Recovery, Inc., for allowing me to learn from them and participate in their group meetings. I cannot thank them enough, nor can I thank them enough nor the organization they represent for sharing some valuable aids in lessening my own load of stress at that time.

I am grateful to the directors of Alcoholics Anonymous World Services, Inc., for permission to print The Twelve Steps as an appendix to my book. Those steps are a key resource for what I have written, and I am deeply indebted to them.

To members of my stress classes, to Barbara Thompson and Dr. A. B. Hardy of TERRAP in Menlo Park,

ACKNOWLEDGMENTS

California; and to Kathy Reese of Weight Watchers.

Most of all, I owe a debt of inestimable gratitude to my husband, Marvin, whose confidence and support have been mine all along the way and whose enthusiastic sales promotion prepared the way for the book to get into the hands of the readers.

Contents

THE PARABLE
OF THE PINE

At the bottom of the hill on which I live, standing by itself at the corner of a hospital's grounds, is a beautiful old Japanese character pine. For five feet or so it emerges in a vertical line from the ground beneath. But then, its trunk bends to almost a forty-five-degree angle in a horizontal line parallel with the ground. There it sends its branches outward and upward toward the sky. I can never pass it without admiring its beauty of line and its unique gracefulness.

I am sure the same process that shapes the Japanese bonsai was used to shape the tree, although the bonsai remains potted in a container, and its roots are cut so as to dwarf the tree. For the natural growth of the pine is upward, straight, and symmetrical.

One day while walking around our hill and in our neighborhood, I passed a home in front of which is a Japanese garden. All the shrubs have been shaped, and one small pine is slowly growing into somewhat the shape of my beloved pine at the foot of the hill. The man who owns the home is a skilled gardener, and I paused to watch how the tree was being shaped by wires fastened to its trunk and anchored beneath the rocky soil to its sturdiest roots. Along its branches are horizontal boards with hooks in either end. These hooks fasten to the wires that go downward to the rock surrounding the taproot. Slowly, as the young pine puts forth new growth, the pulleys attached to the wires are tightened, creating stress between the taproot and the branches above.

From the time the small tree is planted, the grower has in mind a picture of the form he wishes the tree to take. It will be unique. No other tree within sight of it will resemble it in shape or artistry. Passersby will stop to admire its unusual bent form and its beauty.

But suppose, in the process of being bent, the trunk breaks? The gardener needs to know just how much stress the tree can withstand. Deep down in the ground its taproot is firmly planted in the rich soil where the rains and wind cannot dislodge it. Thus the many wires anchored close to the taproot cannot overthrow or uproot the tree, bent though it is.

Herein lies a parable. If too much stress is applied to our lives, or if a storm lashes too strongly against the tree of our being, and if we are too rigid, we may break beyond repair. But if the Master Gardener, the One who does the feeding, the pruning, the shaping, is also the Source of our being, we shall gradually be able to bend without breaking.

And in the end? Who knows but that our lives may become an inspiration to those who are in the process of being formed but who have been bent almost to the breaking point themselves?

Stress:
A Personal Introduction

For many years I have been very involved with the problem of stress and how to handle it. I myself have had a lot of stress with which to deal. But I also know that these days in which I live are stress-laden for almost everyone. Scarcely a family is not touched by stress. And some families and individuals have greater loads of stress than they can handle.

For the sake of clarity, let us differentiate between stress and overstress. Most persons can deal with one stress at a time—it may be a death in the family, the loss of a job, pregnancy, divorce, a change in life-style of a beloved family member—you name it. Though the trauma may be sudden and very heavy, eventually, after weeks or months or perhaps years, some techniques for dealing with it are found, and life goes on. Much depends upon the temperament of the person involved and the inherent biochemistry and genes. However, when a whole set of stress factors occurs within too short a given time, zeroing in on the victim, it may be impossible to deal with the overload of stress, and professional help must be sought. While I have found myself to be in this latter group of the overstressed, most persons fall prey to stresses singly, with the stress factor spaced out into a longer period of time and thus find it more easily dealt with. And if handled wisely, the next stress period does not do as much damage as the first.

Some of the more fortunate among us, born with extremely well integrated central nervous systems and an innate emotional and mental balance, have little trouble rolling with the punches. If your physical body is strong, and if your biochemistry is in order and well balanced, if you sleep well at night, and if you are not too tense and tightly strung nervously, you are fortunate indeed. Some have had more normal childhood experiences and wiser parents than others and have not had to cope with too great a stress load at an early age. Perhaps they just inherited a better set of genes.

I am not a professional counselor and am only an amateur student of psychology; so I cannot speak with authority on the more complex ramifications of the behavioral sciences. However, from the standpoint of my own experience I have learned much about the ways in which stress gets to one and some of the reasons it gets there. In addition, I have made it my business to learn some techniques that help me deal with stress when it is a part of my daily life. I have a great yearning to pass along some of these techniques—in a Christian context—to other strugglers. For in the long run, I have learned that psychology is not enough, and "spiritual awareness" is not enough. It takes a combination of the two to understand the reasons for stress and to give one the wisdom to deal with them, in a lasting and constructive way.

I could discuss in considerable detail my own experiences with stress. I will mention some stresses in the course of the book and also summarize some here. The point I want to underline, from the outset, is that I know about stress from the inside and identify deeply with those who are having trouble coping with it.

As I look back at my own life, there was, first of all, the stress of being the last child after four older brothers. My parents were forty-seven when I was born.

Then there was the extreme religious Fundamentalism of our home. Emphasis on the Fundamentalist theology made its inroads into my highly sensitive being, and I struggled often with a sense of morbid guilt over many a triviality of conduct that might well have been dropped and forgotten. Likewise I developed a huge sense of responsibility for the members of my family, which carried over in later years to the home I was to establish.

Being the only girl in a very male-oriented family, I was early pressed into service as housekeeper while my mother, who was a professional nurse, occasionally accepted cases in towns at some distance from ours. I was left to do the planning, buying, cooking, and keeping of the house—while still keeping up my work at school. One week I was a child, much overprotected by my mother who simply saw no fault in me but who wanted me to be her very special little girl. And the next week I was a woman with the responsibility for the family's food and care.

During the course of my life I have moved to twenty houses. And of that twenty, not one claims the title of "home." Home became where we lived that year. One town where my husband and I lived for twenty-two years is the only place that feels like home; and even there we lived in two different houses. Because of constant moving from place to place, I grew up with a deep feeling of rootlessness insofar as those roots were attached to the ground or to a particular house or even to a community.

When I am aware of parents who do not even want the families they already have, I am incapable of understanding their outlook. As for me, I wanted desperately to have several children and suffered deeply when denied the wish through a series of agonizing losses. I recognize that the population explosion has changed attitudes toward large families. Nonetheless, after my marriage I wanted a family. And so did my husband.

My first pregnancy aborted. Then, I was able to give birth to a very healthy child who survives and has been blessed with good health. Next, a second son was born, earlier than expected and by emergency Cesarean section. Though jaundiced and frail at first, he was apparently a healthy baby. But just before his first birthday he became very ill. It was wartime, and the doctor was trying to attend to several practices. He came too late, the baby died in my arms in an ambulance as I tried to breathe life into him.

Three years later I gave birth to a third child, a little girl. But because of the Rh blood factor, which was not fully understood at that time, she died soon after birth. My dream of a family was shrinking fast.

I sealed myself off. I could not cry; no tears would come. At first I stared at a blank ceiling. And soon I realized that God, who had been my constant companion and so real to me, was not to be found. He had gone off somewhere and forsaken me! I never stopped praying, but the old closeness and feeling of his presence were gone. I wasn't at all sure he even heard my cry.

Within a short time I started dreaming of adopting a baby and soon became so obsessed with the idea that I could talk of doing little else. Not in two years, mind you (the adoption society told us it would take at least that long), but as soon as we could find one for adoption. Any baby, but now! My husband felt we should wait and go through an adoption society, for he knew my own health was precarious. And he knew both my physical and mental health would be better if we were to wait. After all, I had an active six-year-old to take care of. But the obsession of adopting a baby now took possession of me. I was convinced that once the baby was in my arms, I'd be miraculously well again.

A sad train of circumstances followed. My physical health worsened. In less than a year I had experienced pregnancy; a move to a new home with a new school situation for my child and a new job with much greater responsibilities for my husband; major surgery and a severe thyroid imbalance; the death of my baby; my mother, who had been a victim of diabetes and arteriosclerosis, became senile, her memory completely failed, and she had to be placed in a rest home; my child had the measles, and I had to get up night after night with him while I was still recuperating from surgery. Overstress! I could have predicted the result if I had known then what I now know.

At about that time our doctor, in the city from which we had moved and where I had returned to have the baby, phoned to tell us that he had an available ten-day-old baby for us to adopt. We went to the hospital that afternoon and brought the baby home—a beautiful dark-haired girl.

But my feelings were numb; they had gone dead, and I could not get in touch with them. I was trying to force myself to have the feelings of love and acceptance by an act of will. But it doesn't work that way. I, who had thought myself to be God's very special child, was not special at all. And instead of feeling love, I became terribly afraid of . . . I knew not what. That fear led to a general malaise of anxiety that never left me, day or night. I would sleep fifteen minutes or so from sheer exhaustion and then get up and pace the floor. We had not lived in that house long enough for me to feel at home, and the walls seemed strange and unwelcoming. I had not had time to become acquainted with many of the people in our church and had no friends to whom to turn. My husband was swamped with responsibilities in the new and demanding task of ministering to a larger church. Our six-year-old wore me out with his unending activity. And more and more I withdrew into a world of unreality, ending with inevitable breakdown.

As I look at it now, I think much of the trauma and eventual siege of mental and emotional illness could have been avoided. Had I ever trained myself to deal with stress, I might have avoided complete collapse. Who knows? My stress score (see Appendix B) had zoomed to over three hundred, and that is very high, even for a well person.

One does not undergo severe illnesses and many bouts with major and minor surgery without encountering stress. A major thyroid imbalance—also a factor to be reckoned with in a collapse of the nervous system—and finally the involvement of electroshock therapy were the most shattering of all.

One does not lose all the members of a large family (with the exception of one remaining brother) without feeling the loneliness of separation and loss. And one does not lose two of her three children along with the hope of having a large family without the accompanying frustration and grief. Nor does one care for a baby for eighteen months with the hope of adoption and then be forced to give her up, without still further agony.

When I had begun to recuperate but was still very depressed, friends in the church who were also members of Alcoholics Anonymous asked me to go with them to one of their general meetings in San Francisco. I could not understand why they would think I had anything in common with the problems of alcoholics, for I had heretofore thought of them as being "those people," totally unrelated to myself. But I agreed to go. I'd even have given Zen Buddhism or transcendental meditation or yoga a fling, if such avenues of dealing with stress had then been offered! I needed help. I was desperate to get hold of something deeper than and beyond the faith I already held. It had been a lifetime faith, but it had been so inadequate that I had almost lost it in my desperate attempt to hang on to sanity. I had continued to pray, but my prayers didn't get very far. And I was haunted by an ever-present fear of something whose origin I did not know but that kept me from any peace of mind.

I shall never forget that meeting, held in the Coliseum in San Francisco. Bill Wilson, co-founder of Alcoholics Anonymous, had come from the East Coast to be the speaker. In that huge, smoke-filled room I think I have never heard the Lord's Prayer prayed more profoundly or with more meaning. And as that tall, lanky man with the twinkling blue eyes spoke, it was as though God himself reached out addressing every word to me.

When that lecture was over, I was introduced to Bill Wilson; for my friends had known him personally for several years. I found myself relating to him immediately and telling him about my recent struggle with emotional and mental illnesses. Also I found myself spilling out the story of grief over losing my children and my hopelessness of ever recovering my health and of being left with permanent disability.

From his great height he looked down into my eyes and said, "Mrs. Stuart, do you know what we alcoholics call your sort of people? We call you *dry alcoholics.* You're really not all that different from us, only you just never took to the bottle!" Touché! From that day to this I have never looked down on an alcoholic nor considered him or her to be beneath my love and acceptance. There but for the grace of God go I! And I have the greatest respect for the program and the work of Alcoholics Anonymous. Later I shall refer to their Twelve Steps (Appendix B), which are a deeply spiritual approach to dealing with stress. I strongly suggest the use of them in our church group programs. For while they are especially designed for the compulsive drinker, they are indispensable in dealing with more generalized stress. Alcoholics Anonymous has the longest and finest record of any of the secular agencies around the world for dealing with alcoholism. I think if I could qualify, I'd be a member.

Nineteen forty-three and 1944 proved to be my years of greatest overstress. I might say that the years since then have been productive, and I have learned to live with stress and surmount most of its ravages. My nervous system took a beating that it will not allow me to forget. I thank God, however, that I am alive and eager for life.

There have been other times when the stress thermometer registered a high score, and my state of anxiety and depression rose with it. A move from one part of the country to another, along with other personal factors at that time, caused mounting stress, and I felt I needed some skilled help in dealing with it. When a counselor friend of mine in southern California suggested that I look into the possibility of attending a group for people with nervous problems, known as Recovery, Inc., I found one near my home and began attending. There I went faithfully for nine months, receiving much personal help and learning the technique originated by the founder, Dr. Abraham Low, of Evanston, Illinois, in the 1950s.

I have discovered, in studying several methods and techniques of secular groups for dealing with stress, that they are all eclectic—that is, they borrow from one another. This is even true of the writers of the Bible who, beginning with the Hebrew, borrowed from the Romans and the Greeks and, later, from many other peoples. True, each group has certain distinguishing characteristics. But each appears to have something valuable to lend. There are now at least twenty-five or more groups that are registered units of the Human Growth Potential Movement, and I daresay each has borrowed something from another.

I have learned that a succession of stressful events within a short period of time can throw the strongest person into a feeling of helplessness and hopelessness. It is at this point that a weekly stress group whose orientation is that of the Christian faith and practice could be of inestimable support and help. It is my conviction that this is what the church of Jesus Christ must provide and nurture. Its leaders must be trained and experienced and, above all, possessed of a deep and abiding faith as well as a strong sense of dedication. We must reach out to our troubled ones and give them help when they need it.

I know that such groups can work—and work well. Years after my breakdown I started with a beloved group of younger women that we named Anx Anon. For two years we met regularly just to share our concerns and give one another support. Then, I started extending that experience to other groups, in shorter periods of time, and have found the effort most successful. I do not pose as a professional here. But that is what encourages me most: if I can provide help for others who experience overstress, then many, many others can provide similar help also.

I do not envision a standard structure for such groups in all locations, though it would be tempting to propose such a structure. But I have adapted one outlined in Appendix C, based upon my experience in teaching the groups for which I have been the leader. This might be a model for any such groups desiring an effective starting point. The combination of techniques, drawn from various sources, contains nothing startlingly innovative, so far as I know. But it illustrates what can be done in a group of ordinary church people, nonprofessionals, with a little help from the outside.

In succeeding chapters, with the possibility of forming local church support groups clearly in mind, I want to share insights that have come to me through a variety of experiences. Those insights, I hope, will be helpful to individuals seeking personal guidance and to those who, in addition, may want to form networks of communication with others suffering from stress. In that sharing, I hope to continue my own journey with increased resources for sensitivity and understanding.

Up the Down Staircase

The title of this chapter comes from the title of a well-known book by Bel Kaufman. It deals with the stress and strain of a young Brooklyn high-school teacher in coping with the problems of a class of English students in a very troubled and run-down section of the city. In the old building there was a double stairway, one for the down traffic and the other for those going up. Her life was so full of ups and downs that she often found herself headed up the down stairway when she should have been going down. She was teaching a group of students unlike any she had ever known before; many of them were as old or older than she; the problem of discipline was great, and she did not have a lot of support from her administrator; she knew her subject, but often she found great gaps in the learning of her students that made it impossible to present the material in a knowledgeable way. The rule of thumb had been "force, intimidate, but do not be so foolish as to appreciate." And her approach was entirely different. Yet, she chose to live with the discomfort in order to encourage her students to respect learning and to respect the one who brought it to them.

While stress, or an overload of stress, can attack anyone, regardless of the personality or nervous system involved, it finds ready victims among the up-the-down-stairs temperaments. These persons are geared to a greater sensitivity, a shorter fuse, than others, and they often lack objectivity.

People irritate us, and we do not respond positively. Our body sensations might be described somewhat as the jagged ups and downs of an electrocardiogram rather than the smooth undulations of a flowing river. You can well imagine, if you don't know firsthand, what this situation does to the sleeping habits of many a person. Can you picture yourself sleeping on a pegboard? Or, have you gone on a camping trip and tried to make yourself comfortable in a sleeping bag, only to discover after everyone else was asleep that you were lying on a series of roots that kept jabbing you from underneath? And you couldn't get comfortable any way you moved? You just had to lie quiet and not disturb the others, but *you* didn't sleep. Or, if you did, it was intermittent, and your mind kept waking up even if your body was still.

Family members irritate you. Your husband keeps leaving doors open as he goes out of the room, letting in a blast of cold air behind him. You ask him brusquely, "Were you raised in a barn?" Your son has a habit of scratching his head or rubbing his nose, and you keep averting your eyes when in conversation with him so as not to see him do it. Your daughter bites her nails, and you think there won't possibly be anything left of them to protect her from the cruel world. Maybe your aging mother has lost considerable weight after acquiring false teeth, and they don't fit any longer. And every time she bites there is a slight click of those teeth. You think, "I cannot face this meal, let alone three meals a day with this annoyance!" You glower but don't want to hurt her feelings. And the next meal is the same old story. You find your whole nervous system responding like a taut-stringed instrument, and you are unable to relax and let go of your inner tensions. What is more, you seem to have a need to try to control everyone around you.

This is how you are built. This is the *essential* you. Add to this temperament a number of stressful events and situations in your life bringing a demand for adjustment and change, and you find yourself unable or even helpless in coping with life and feeling quite hopeless about it all. You can't control the people in your environment. You can't change the environment, and you can't control you.

I was talking the other day with the young man who cuts my hair, and we were discussing a study I've been making about stress techniques. He commented, "But I don't understand why a person who decides to quit smoking or drinking or any habit for that matter can't just quit." Ah, there's the rub. A few persons can, but most persons can't. There's the matter of compulsive behavior.

In Romans 7:14-25, Paul says:

My own behaviour baffles me. For I find myself doing what I really loathe but not doing what I really want to do. Yet surely if I do things that I really don't want to do, I am admitting that I really agree that the Law is good. But it cannot be said that "I" am doing them at all. . . . I often find that I have the will to do good, but not the power. That is, I don't accomplish the good I set out to do, and the evil I don't really want to do I find I am always doing. Yet if I do things that I don't really want to do then it is not, I repeat,

"I" who do them, but the sin which has made its home within me. My experience of the Law is that when I want to do good, only evil is within my reach. ... It is an agonising situation, and who can set me free from the prison of this mortal body?

Paul didn't know what the conscious and the subconscious minds were, not in psychological terms. But he experienced the battle of the conscious mind versus the unconscious and struggled with it intermittently all his days. Even after his dramatic conversion, when his life became completely committed to the doing of God's will, he was tripped up again and again by this struggle he called Sin. If you are compulsive in behavior, you know what I'm talking about. One part of you sincerely desires to go in one direction, and another part of you pulls in the opposite direction. When the struggle becomes too intense, nervous fatigue results. And what is nervous fatigue, or exhaustion? A sickness not of the mind or of the emotion but a sickness of the *will*. The very thing you've been trying so hard to control will no longer do your bidding.

The person who operates the central control system of your life has resigned, walked off the job, and left no one at the switchboard. Members of Alcoholics Anonymous have a way of smiling at the problem drinker who still hangs on to the idea that he can control his drinking. "Let him try," they say. "If he has any method possible for controlling his drinking, let him employ it; he's not for us." But they know eventually he'll be crying for help. So it is with the person victimized by nervous fatigue or confused by a too-high-scoring load of stress. You find that the harder you try the worse you get. You are going in six different directions at one time, and you are confused. You debate the rightness or wrongness of your motives, and helplessness results. If this goes on long enough, you become frightened that you'll never be able to gain control, and panic results. Or you struggle with uncontrollable obsessions or fantasies. You are the victim of your own unruly emotions and are allowing yourself to be ruled by your feelings rather than by your will.

To press the point further: Are you convinced that you are totally a victim of your temperament? At one time I think I might have bought that idea, but I now realize that most of us are both victim and instigator. Again and again I catch myself prolonging the agony of my depressed feelings by my negative outlook. I won't let go because if I find myself to be wrong in holding to the feelings I have, I might be plunging out into never-never land, and I fear that the essential "I" will get lost in the shuffle. And as much as I hesitate to admit it, there are times when my subconscious appears to enjoy suffering and flagellation. These are times when I find it hard to muster enough faith to believe that there is something better ahead and that this too shall pass away.

In the well-known best seller *How to Be Your Own Best Friend,* one of William Faulkner's characters is quoted as saying, "Between grief and nothing, I'll take grief." And the author goes on to say:

> But our choice is between grief and discomfort—and a fuller life. To take the first steps toward that life may be painful, and you have to endure sharp pangs of loneliness and loss. But you've always been a bit lonely and your loss may have happened a long time ago. What you are losing

now is only a dream. (Mildred Newman and Bernard Berkowitz [New York: Random House, 1973], p. 38)

We all tend to want life served up to order, don't we? We turn wistfully to the person who suggests the sort of discipline it will take to put us in running order, and then we turn away, sadly. Our answer is "Yes, but you see, I just haven't the time" or "I'm not quite sure this method is the best one for me" or "This program won't fit into my schedule." What we are actually saying is, "I could possibly do this, but I don't want to do it enough to make the effort. And I don't want to change my mind."

We of the past and present generations have been infused with the concept of comfort. Compared to previous generations we lead very comfortable lives. Our system is based on it. We desire frequent smorgasbords of discipline—a bit of knowledge, a new insight here and there—but no hourly or daily grubbing, thank you! We'd rather pay the psychiatrist to do our thinking for us and be our father or mother confessor than try to find out what God wants us to do and then dig out the hard stones of discipline until we hit the solid earth underneath us. We'd rather have scapegoats, such as our meager childhood or our parents who didn't understand us and conditioned us to be the way we are. Or sex, for instance. You can hang almost anything you do or don't do on the excuse that you haven't had a satisfactory sex life.

"Make me happy," we cry. "Soothe my troubled feelings." "Massage me; feed me; bring me my morning newspaper, and don't ask me to speak to you in a civil manner before nine in the morning!" On our street there is a minimum of two automobiles for each family, with numerous vans, pickup trucks, motor homes, and motorcycles interspersed here and there. In our kitchen there are all the electrical appliances we need or can use and sometimes more. In some homes, microwave ovens are replacing the older, more conventional ones. We are so used to the idea of ease and physical support and comfort that we cannot accept the personal discipline involved in tapering down our style of living, unless untoward circumstances force us to do so. Our television programs have convinced us that the easy way is the best way. Crash diets bring our poundage down, but we do not usually keep it that way. Rigid fasting for a period of time or diet pills as a short-time routine give way to riotous, undisciplined eating, and in time obesity again haunts us. We believe that skill may be learned by six easy lessons and send our daughters to their young husbands with no training in cooking or in housekeeping skills. No wonder so many marriages break up! Good food well balanced and well cooked holds the key to more successful marriages than we would care to admit. But most of us will not set ourselves to the task of self-discipline in learning the necessary skills week after week, month after month, year after year.

But here you are. And here I am. The person at the controls has departed, and we're facing in all directions at one time. We have been told that at the base of emotional or mental health there has to be a recognition of one's helplessness and a commitment to seek help beyond ourselves. There has to be a belief that the help is there, even if at the time we cannot see where it is or how it is to work or who our helper is. Help is there, if we can only get in touch with it.

If you are now feeling a great deal of inner stress

because of outer-stress problems, there is no easy road to mental or emotional health—or spiritual health either. It's taken a long time for you and me to get ourselves into the state we're in. Many of us were born with this rather highly strung temperament, and much of what has happened to us since birth has not made it any easier for us to live with ourselves. In many cases the overload of stress has been too great. But if you are obsessed with a demand for comfort, forget it! How much comfort did Paul have during the course of his lifetime, especially *after* his conversion? How much comfort did Jesus of Nazareth have in the three years of his brief public ministry? In each case comfort was missing, but each person had the inner comfort of knowing he was doing the will of God—and had a clear conscience, yes, and had the respect of close and valued friends who trusted their lives with their leader's direction because of his integrity and purpose and because they could see God the Father in what was happening.

We demand miracles; we cry out for wholeness; we want it all in one fell swoop. We forget we must pay a price for it. That's the basic ingredient Alcoholics Anonymous teaches its followers: that they will always have a craving for the comfort and exhilaration of alcohol but be unable to take so much as one drink without surrendering their sobriety. Their allergy, illness, obsession—whatever their particular problem— will never leave them. One drink will be too many; yet all the drinks in the world won't be enough. Their problem may be arrested but never permanently cured. So it is with obese persons and an abundance of the wrong sort of food. They will have to fight the problem of obesity for the rest of their life. Even if they become trim and slim, they will have to fight the obsession of overeating, for they are susceptible and may slip right back into the habit of gorging themselves or comforting themselves with food at the slightest provocation.

I can recall our Weight Watchers leader's saying, "The most important thing in my whole life is to stay slim." At the time I thought she was overdramatizing her problem, because I could think of any one of a dozen factors more important to me than my being fat or thin. However, she realized that she couldn't live with herself if she slipped back. What's more, she would lose her job. And I am sure that's the way it is with the alcoholic. It's the way it is with the former mental or psychoneurotic person. Your mental health has to become a matter of daily concern and practice, for if you relapse, you are of no use to yourself or to anyone else. And so we all must develop the will to be uncomfortable.

How do I know? Because I have experienced nervous illness, overstress, great inner discomfort, and have had to find a way of dealing with it. What I have learned has not come from books, nor is it a suggestion picked at random out of another person's experience. It has happened to me, and I have had to struggle with finding an answer. I struggle constantly, for the up-the-down-staircase temperament is mine for good. I can never totally escape the discomfort of it.

However, I, like the alcoholic, know I cannot solve my problems alone, nor can I deal with compulsive behavior alone. Nevertheless, I *do* know, with God's help, I can. He is able! I know this from experience. If you will accept his requirements for inner discipline with every temptation, with every sorrow, with every calamity that may happen to you, some extra strength will be given to you as a means of coping with it. Stress need not break you: it can provide the impetus for growth greater than any you have ever known, provided you allow God to direct your life.

Evelyn Miller Berger, daughter of Bishop Miller of The United Methodist Church and a consulting psychologist, was of more help than anyone else to me at the time of my psychoneurosis. I recall talking with her one day and crying out in great distress, "I simply can't go on this way; if there isn't a miracle or unless something happens to me to help me out of this hole, I am sure I shall lose my mind!" When I had got beyond the panic and calmed down a bit she quietly asked, "And what if God does not choose to perform a miracle, Mary Ella, what then?" She went on to help me see that everyone carries a cross. And often the cross people bear is unusually heavy. Mine was one for which I was not responsible and one I had not chosen. But could I escape it? She suggested that God had already promised help for today. "As thy day, so shall thy strength be." I could get through this day without falling on my face or infecting my family members with my anxiety and depressed feelings. Then, at night, I could turn over the reins to God while I slept, knowing that when I awakened I could reach out and take hold of the promise of strength for today, once again. Then she asked me to put that acceptance of my heavy load into a prayer and tell God that's what I intended to do. No miracle happened; no load was automatically lifted; but gradually day after day and week after week, I began to have more good days than bad. And I was able to get out of the morass of my despair.

Lines from the closing paragraph of Leo Rosten's novel *Captain Newman, M.D.* come to mind:

> Then Newman said, "My father once told a story I always think of when the going gets rough and things look hopeless. It's about Destiny. . . . Destiny came down to an island centuries ago and summoned three of its inhabitants before him. "What would you do," asked Destiny, "if you were told that tomorrow this island will be completely inundated by an immense tidal wave?"
>
> The first man, who was a cynic, said, "Why I would eat, drink, carouse, and make love all night long." The second man who was a mystic, said, "I would go to the sacred grove with my loved ones and make sacrifices to the gods and pray without ceasing." And the third man who loved reason, thought a while, confused and troubled, and said, "Why, I would assemble our wisest men and begin at once to study how to live under water!" ([New York: Harper & Brothers], p. 331)

Adjust or perish! Learn to live with discomfort. We must make it our companion; this is the first step. If we would handle the inevitable stress from the outside that all too often presses in from many different sources, we must first learn to cope with the inner stress that tears us apart and allows no peace of mind. In accepting and then absorbing the pain of discomfort, we shall also see that in a sense we have prolonged the agony. In the beginning we were not consciously responsible for our response to inner stress. But in accepting it we are now commissioned to do something about it.

In the words of Dr. Howard Thurman, whom I met during his ministry in California: "The test of life often is found in the amount of pain you can absorb without losing your joy." This is the secret, isn't it? To carry a cross does not mean to let it break your back but to hold it high as the crucifier carries it at the head of a church procession. Thus it becomes a symbol of victory, and only then can it do its redeeming work. You absorb its spirit, and it becomes a part of your being but only if you refuse to allow that cross to steal from you your joy!

If It Feels Good

If it feels good, do it! That is a concept of our day that appears again and again in our modern verbiage. "I'm comfortable with that," someone will say, or "How do you feel about that?" rather than "What do you *think* about that?" These expressions represent the present-day attempt to get in touch with our feelings which for so many generations have been somewhat submerged in our very strong sense of duty and in our doing or not doing something just because we think it might be more in accordance with what is expected by our elders rather than our doing it or not because it *feels* right or wrong.

A part of this emphasis is a good thing, I think, but the concept of forming our value judgments on the basis of whether it feels good can also lead to chaos. Always and always we Americans seem to swing as a pendulum from one side to the other, and I think we are now at the end of the swing (or close to it, I hope) of the do-it-because-it-feels-good pendulum. For if feeling is not tempered by fact, one is in deep trouble.

My husband and I had an example of the extremity of acting on emotion alone, this past Fourth of July. On our street there are many early college-aged and younger teen-aged youths. About a week before the Fourth of July the parents of those youths took off to the mountains and left their children to "take care of the place" while they were gone. Motorcycles raced back and forth up and down our hill late at night and even in the early morning hours. High explosives placed under bottles were set off, scattering glass everywhere on the street and into the lawns. One small girl was burned on the hand and an explosive singed the back of her hair. The neighbors on the street who did not have teen-agers were momentarily at a loss to know what to do, for the parents were away. When one of the parents finally came back home the youths were sent to sweeping the street and cleaning up the broken glass and beer cans strewn everywhere. But, the incident has not been forgotten. It was an orgy that affected everyone on the street, for it plainly demonstrated the fact that if you do what feels good and have no consideration for the fact that others live on that street and are entitled to some consideration, there will be peace for no person there.

Now I realize that every one of us who grew from youth to adulthood had moments of abandon without thought or consideration for the rights of other persons, just "letting it all hang loose" or doing what felt good. A certain amount of reckless bravado is to be expected. But, as I observe the situation today, I see more violence, less respect for older persons and authority figures, less taking into account the ultimate goals, and a greater emphasis on the now than I have known in the past. There appears to be less responsibility on the part of parents, considering them on the whole. Perhaps we are all reaping the irresponsibilities of Vietnam and of

Watergate. And we are dealing with the results of overuse of drugs and alcohol by many persons who make up our society, coupled with a so-what, devil-may-care attitude toward tradition.

However, we must attempt to understand the matter of "feelings versus facts" on a personal level before we can even attempt to do anything about the problem on a social level. It is quite necessary, I think, for all of us to know why we feel as we do and why we so often respond to life situations on a feeling level rather than on one of facing facts.

Take a panic reaction, for example. Your husband was expected home from a night meeting at about ten-thirty. It is now eleven-thirty and no husband. You telephone the place where the meeting was held, but there is no answer. You wait another thirty minutes, your stress level rising all the time. You have a dry mouth and your heart is beating rapidly. Your imagination conjures up all sorts of automobile accidents: your man is an excellent driver, but how about the irresponsible drivers on the highway who have had one drink too many? Also, what about a heart attack? One of your best friends lost her husband in just such a way, coming home from a workout at a nearby health club; he could scarcely steer the car to the side of the road, and the motor stopped before the fatal blood clot reached his heart. Your imagination races wildly, jumping from one awful possibility to another. Then the thought comes to you: Why didn't I go with him? I could have shared the driving, and maybe he wouldn't have gone to sleep at the wheel.

Downstairs you hear the car come into the garage, and your husband appears at the foot of the stairs. He is safe, as you can see, but you glower and say, "For heaven's sake, what happened?" You learn that the meeting was a half hour later closing than was expected. And then, on the way home a three-car accident had tied up traffic for almost an hour. But you are left with disturbed emotions and a racing pulse. And your sleep is intermittently disturbed by wild dreams and nightmares.

What to do about such a panic situation, you ask? Just this sort of panic reaction has occurred to me again and again. The situation is always different, but the reaction somewhat the same. My husband's job requires much traveling, and I have had to learn ways of dealing with the inevitable emergencies that ensue.

First of all, I realize that such panic makes my imagination immediately run wild. I become almost completely subjective and unable to concentrate. So, the task at hand is to get the imagination calmed down and my subjective feelings to subside so as to sort out the facts in the situation. I realize that he is a good driver and is in excellent health and that meetings do often run overtime. With this realization I also recall that whenever he is to be considerably later than I expect, he almost always manages to telephone. Since he has not done so, there must have been some extenuating circumstance, and a telephone is not available at the moment.

This is not comforting; but it is a fact, nevertheless. Then I tell myself that he has always arrived eventually and safely. And I try to think of the overwhelming ratio of drivers on the road to those involved directly in accident. If I can objectify my feelings, removing any stored up or hidden resentment about this fly-by-night existence of ours that involves so much travel and so much actual risk, I become calmer. In any panic situation, I know the subjective feelings must be brought to the surface and made objective. And this can be done only by changing my thoughts and looking at the facts involved.

Thousands of people wake up every morning with a feeling of dread and even terror at having to face a new day and its demands. By midmorning, perhaps, the worst symptoms fade, and by midafternoon acute anxiety is gone. But the next morning again brings the old anxious feeling and the uncertainty about what to do with it. Still thousands of others cannot go to sleep at night without a sedative. Others go off to sleep but wake in three or four hours, finding themselves unable to go back to sleep again. A few persons are so built that they can exist with a few hours of sleep; but most of us cannot.

Anxiety occurs—said the late Dr. Leslie Weatherhead, a greatly admired and beloved clergyman and writer from London—when one's self-esteem is threatened (*Prescription for Anxiety* [Nashville: Abingdon Press, 1968], p. 5). For example, it may occur when the desire to do something or to realize some cherished ambition conflicts with the fear that it cannot be done. One part of the mind says, "Yes! This is what I've always wanted, always dreamed of but in my wildest imaginings never thought I'd have a chance at." At the same time, another part of the mind whispers, "Run! You're not up to it! In fact, you can't possibly do it! Someone with much more ability who is stronger and smarter than you, will have the chance. But you're not up to it!" Inner struggle gives way to confusion. And if this confusion is not taken care of by decisive action, the conflict will not be settled.

44

Then, if the unexpected happens, and there's a turn of affairs that makes the choice not viable, you are left with a recurring, nagging feeling that you are not adequate after all.

In the church there are those who point the guilty finger at the anxiety-laden persons who have become incapable of decisive action. And this, of course, makes the anxiety all the greater. You have the deep-seated feeling that your faith ought to make you strong enough to stand up and fight the anxious feelings. But you have not the physical or emotional strength. The person at the switchboard is asleep, and there's no one in control.

It is well, I think, to often remind yourself that negative feelings cannot be controlled by act of will. True, the resulting action can eventually be controlled and can be trained to result in positive procedure. But the feeling itself cannot be controlled. For example, you cannot will to feel loving toward a certain person, not at all. You can will to have goodwill toward that person and treat him or her in a loving way. But you cannot control the feeling. Only the thought connected with the feeling can be changed and eventually controlled. Strong or overwhelming feelings may come at any time of day or night with physical symptoms as accompaniment: the dry mouth; the wildly beating pulse; the tight band around the head, causing constant headache—all these and many other well-known symptoms keep churning inside you. It takes a persistently strong person to train the mind that there is no imminent peril attached to these symptoms. They seem so real!

On a less neurotic level, most of us, in dealing with an overload of stress or even a moderately stressful situation, act on the impulse of our feelings rather than taking the time and effort to sort out the facts involved. We immediately become subjective, filtering the situation through the sieve of our imagination rather than through the positive approach of fact. Old patterns, long buried in our subconscious mind, repeat themselves and are brought up to the conscious mind as though they had happened only yesterday. These may come all the way from early childhood, but while we are in an upset state of mind, we do not recognize them as such. We play them over and over in our mind with our negative feeling responding in kind. Our imagination becomes distorted; we become incapable of keeping our cool and of reacting positively to the situation at hand. Or, we interpret another's reaction toward us and start imagining all sorts of feelings that may not even be in the mind of that person at all. If we project our feelings upon someone near and dear to us and imagine that what we are feeling toward that person at the moment is what he or she is feeling toward us, possibly even magnified, we are allowing feeling and not fact to dominate our reason. When we become upset and allow our feelings to be magnified but do not go about finding out the facts in the case by laying all the cards on the table and then talking the situation over with the person involved, we become entrenched in the camp of our own subjective feelings and at war with each other. Or, we remain aloof in cold silence of withdrawal, completely unable to make any exchange of viewpoint at all.

I know from experience that there are situations that demand days, weeks, months, possibly years, to really be worked through. These are the hardest to live with. We humans demand immediate answers and the resolution of our tensions, but God says, "Wait!" Our time schedule is not in alignment with his, and a sort of locking of horns sets in on our part. If we are sincerely trying to do the will of God, we may be patient enough to wait. I am not a patient person, but I have learned that God understands my humanness at this point and puts up with my stubbornness in wanting things to run on my time schedule. In the meantime I have learned I must often remind myself that the only thing in this world that I can be reasonably certain of is change. This, too, shall pass away. And the thing I wanted so desperately last year might not have been good for me or for those I love, and there might be a better way. It takes time for persons to change, to become more loving, more unselfish, more tolerant. Especially is that true for me! Sometimes when I desire others in my life to change, I find that it is I who must do the changing. And that is hard for a stubborn, self-willed person to do. Often only God's grace can bring about that change, and it must come in his time and in his way, not mine.

In a given situation I may think, on the basis of the knowledge I have at hand, that I am also in touch with my feelings. But, have I actually based my feelings on what are truly the facts in the case? This I must do. Then, I must make a decision as to what my attitude will be in regard to the facts I know to be true. There may be many facts that will have to remain in the column of the unknown, for in every situation one cannot possibly know all the facts. I may have imagined many things to be true, especially if I have been given an intuitive mind that can easily fit the pieces of a jigsaw puzzle together. Sometimes this sort of mind can be a curse rather than a blessing because of our human fallibility. One missing piece or one not fitting perfectly may throw the picture entirely out of focus. The facts I am not certain about must be tossed in the discard pile until more light on the subject establishes them as facts. Then I must make a decision to act upon the known facts.

Well-known psychologist Eric Fromm gives his readers an example of freedom of choice involved in making a decision. And he chooses to illustrate in a decision between smoking and not smoking.

Let us take a heavy smoker who has read the reports on the health hazards of smoking and has arrived at the conclusion that he wants to stop smoking. He has "decided that he is going to stop." This "decision" is no decision. It is nothing but the formulation of a hope. He has "decided" to stop smoking, yet the next day he feels in too good a mood, the day after in too bad a mood, the third day he does not want to appear "asocial," the following day he doubts that the health reports are correct, and so he continues smoking, although he had "decided" to stop. All these decisions are nothing but ideas, plans, fantasies; they have little or no reality until the real choice is made. This choice becomes real when he has a cigarette in front of him and has to decide whether to smoke *this* cigarette or not; again, later he has to decide about another cigarette, and so on. It is always the concrete act which requires a decision. The question in each such situation is whether he is free not to smoke, or whether he is not free.

Several questions arise here. Assuming he did not believe in the health reports on smoking or, even if he did, he is convinced that it is better to live twenty years less than to miss this pleasure; in this case there is apparently no problem of choice. Yet the problem may be only camouflaged. His conscious thoughts may be nothing but rationalizations of his feeling that he could not win the battle even if he tried; hence he may prefer to pretend there is no battle to win. But whether the problem of choice is conscious or unconscious, the nature of the choice is the same. It is the choice between an action which is dictated by reason against an action which is dictated by irrational passions. (*The Heart of Man: Its Genius for Good and Evil* [New York: Harper & Row, 1964])

My husband has a good technique for making decisions. When a decision must be made and a course of action agreed upon, he uses a "force-field" approach. After carefully considering alternate courses of action, he leaves an option to one of two decisions. With a sheet of paper in front of him, he draws a line down the middle, making left and right columns. In the left he lists all the reasons in favor of one of the two options, and in the right he does the same for the second course of action. Having already considered the very worst thing that might happen if either course were taken, he searches his mind to ascertain whether he could live with the shock or the pain of that worst, should it happen. He considers the best that could happen. Then he carefully weighs the left-hand items against the right-hand and makes his decision accordingly. Once the decision is made, he is not one to waver or turn back. He does not waste emotion on afterthoughts but goes on to the next item on the agenda. This is not to say that he always makes the right decision. Nor does it say he never wishes he had made a different decision. He is fallible, and he knows it. But he is able to live with his decisions nonetheless.

When a decision is to be made the matter of priorities has to be taken into account along with ultimate goals as opposed to immediate goals. Now and then I find it helpful to sit down with paper and pencil and make a list of priorities with such goals in mind.

In a little autograph book I was given at the time of my high-school graduation, my father, who was often a stranger to me, wrote these words from Shakespeare's *Hamlet*:

> To thine own self be
> true,
> And it must follow, as the night the
> day,
> Thou canst not then be false to any
> man.

At the time I thought this was a rather cold and unfeeling response to my graduation, and I much preferred the more personal warmth of the loving words my mother had written. However, as the years have come and gone, I realize that my father was referring me to a great truth that would be a guide all my life if I could get hold of it. Today I cherish those lines more than I can say. It is one thing to feel, but it is quite another to know.

Coming In Second

Being a perfectionist by nature, I have found it difficult all my life to accept failure. This need to achieve and to be right was abetted by my adoring mother who was a bit blind and unrealistic about her only daughter. I am sure she had no idea whatsoever of the pressure she placed upon me to achieve or she'd never have done it. She really loved me. But many of her dreams had been thwarted, and I suppose she saw in me a chance to bring about the accomplishment that life and the limitation of opportunity had denied her.

For one thing, she was eager to make a public speaker of me. I always liked dramatics and took part in school plays with a great deal of eagerness. And by the time I got to high school, I had learned, with my mother's own coaching, to give dramatic readings. Our small–high-school contestants each year entered in the county contests and track meets. We had few participants and only two gold medalists: a low hurdler, and a dramatic reader—myself. For three years this winning of gold medals went on, and then in my senior year we were moved to a different town. Entering the county contest in this particular town meant that I would compete with students from several large high schools, one with a drama department and a special coach for dramatic readings.

With one part of me I wanted greatly to enter that contest and win a fourth gold medal to round out my high-school accomplishments. But with the other part of me I was afraid and drew back from the challenge. After fighting with myself for weeks over whether I would enter the contest, I finally decided to do so. My mother persuaded me that I would be greatly disappointed in myself if I backed out of the contest, failing to even try. It would be better to fail, she thought, than to refuse to try. I knew she was right, and so I finally found the courage to enter.

When the contest was finished, I knew I had done well. But to my amazement, when the judge's decision was announced, I had come in second rather than first! This was about like coming in last, and I felt myself to be a terrible failure. My mother tried to console me and tell me it was better to have come in second than not to have placed at all. However, that afternoon at the track meet it was announced that the scores of the judges of the Declamatory Contest had been tallied incorrectly, and I had won the coveted gold medal after all. Once again my perfectionist self-esteem was restored. I was a winner!

It must have been at that time that the idea jelled in my mind that life would be like that. You'd have to discipline yourself, of course, and you'd have to be courageous even when you were likely to fail. But if you worked extra hard, and if you could manage to get God on your team, you'd stand to win every time. I couldn't have been more mistaken!

Let me make one thing clear. I shall always be grateful to my mother for insisting that I not give up in defeat on public speaking. To have done so would have made it impossible to speak in public later on when my life demanded so many times that I do so. What is more, I think I would have given up in defeat at other points rather than fighting a thing through to the finish. She knew that. I did not thank her at the time, but I have thanked her since. Still, there was a negative side to that dominant drive to come out on top.

How much more realistic to have anticipated a certain amount of failure. And how much better to respond positively to the denial of some of life's fondest wishes by planning an alternative course. I have seen doors close behind me, never to open again, and I have not always been a good loser. I still hate to fail! In the meantime I have learned some of the causes of this totally unrealistic drive to succeed. And I am beginning to be able to work out a philosophy and some techniques for dealing with some of life's second bests.

What causes perfectionism? First of all, I think it is an inability—or even more, an unwillingness—to accept yourself as you are. Out of this basic lack of acceptance there grows a dissatisfaction with your environment and the persons who make up that environment. In essence, it is a lack of acceptance of life itself on any other terms but your own.

In the beginning this lack of acceptance may spring from an uncertainty about your own identity, or it may spring from a lack of security with your parents or your home situation. If you have been indulged and made to feel that life is easy and going your way, you tend to believe that life will always be like that. On the other hand, if you do not feel you have a place of real significance or importance, you may spend your entire life overachieving, just to prove that your family is wrong and you are right. If your parents just accepted you and enjoyed you for the person you actually are, you would have little trouble adjusting to life.

Favoritism on the part of parents for one child over another accounts for some degree of perfectionism. It also causes the favorite child to get the idea that God makes special allowances for him or her that would not be made otherwise for another less favored. The unfavored one can also become a perfectionist in order to establish the status for which he or she so deeply longs. If you know you do not come first in the hearts of the persons you love the most, perhaps you can win that love and attention by overachieving!

In either case the perfectionist needs to manipulate the people about him or her as well as to exercise a certain control over the surrounding environment. By bringing about a bit of change here and a little adjustment there, we picture-straighteners think we can succeed in bringing the picture into focus for ourselves, whether or not it pleases anyone else.

Perfectionism, I think, could well be called the God complex. But a God complex presupposes perfect physical health and stamina, a rugged nervous system, a keen mind, and an extra dose of common sense with accompanying good judgment. This proves to be an almost impossible formula for most of us. Mind over matter can work only up to a certain point and no further. It also presupposes a perfect environment.

What are some changes perfectionists need to make in their attitudes and response to life?

Let's begin with the home. If you are a parent, it is most necessary that you refuse to play favorites with your children. It is true that a parent may find one child more appealing and easier to relate to than another. But this may be all the more reason for spending extra time with the one most unlovable. One child may possess most of your worst characteristics, and when you are around that child, you are reminded of your own failures. But this is one of the lovable oddities of life and must not necessitate your disliking this child simply because you cannot accept yourself.

I think it is very important that no child in the home ever be allowed to come between husband and wife. I think the role of being a parent must not supersede that of being a husband or wife. Likewise, one child must not be played as a pawn against another or be compared to another. Each child has beautiful qualities of his or her own and must be accepted as being unique and not a standard for another.

Parents need to face honestly the question, Am I trying to achieve through a child a goal that I myself cannot hope to attain? This is manipulation and cannot be allowed. In still another sense, husbands and wives try to manipulate each other through their children. This will always be detected as phony and will be unsuccessful, in the end. It is a facet of perfectionism and must be tossed into the discard. We must learn to accept persons as they are.

Another question must be asked: Do I expect too much of my mate, of my children, or of the persons I am closely associated with? Do I expect special favors without giving favors in return? Do I ask for outstanding achievement on the part of persons with whom I am associated, not taking into account the matter of human failure? No person can possibly be God. It is, however, possible to be special to someone rather than to be exceptional in achievement or perfect.

If you have certain compulsive perfectionist patterns that interfere with a relationship or even that make you unhappy with yourself, start working to disrupt them. Are you willing to settle for less perfection in your own performance in order to spend more time with the people you love? We must discover our priorities, I think, in this pursuit of perfectionism. What matters most? That everything is orderly and our environment is safe and secure? Our personal comfort? Or the relationships with persons we love?

If you, as I, have found that you have not always been a gold medalist but rather that you had to come in second, you might take an objective look at the final result—as of the present. If your first choice had been granted, would it really have worked out for the best for all concerned? Is there any real value in coming in second? I think so. Certainly we human beings need to succeed sometimes and fail at other times. If the emphasis can be on *being* rather than on doing or achieving or arriving, I think we shall be in a much better position to accept life as it is.

The sovereign technique in dealing with perfectionism, I think, is a sense of humor. Just being able to look at the perfectionists we are somehow restores our perspective and helps us appreciate our delightful oddities. God must really chuckle over us at times. We get so deadly serious and demand that his time schedule fit ours. And like little children we stamp our feet and demand to have our way. But he sees the beginning and the ending and all that is lying in between. And so he allows us to dangle for a time while he decides what's best for us.

Demanding perfect performance in ourselves so often keeps us from seeing the delightful possibilities in others. Rarely are we surprised in discovering a veritable diamond in the rough among those who cross our path. And it's because we're expecting too much.

Stop and think with me about your favorite people. Are they all gold medalists? Mine are not. As I think of it now, the ones I actually love the most are far from being winners. They have certain areas in which they excel. But as I see them now in my mind's eye, I see a man gifted in mind and personality who for seven years was a hopeless alcoholic. He was able to get help and help himself, and for many years he and his wife have given full time to Alcoholics Anonymous, to mental health studies, and to the National Foundation for Alcoholic Studies, of which he was president for two years. I see a beautiful woman whose young husband was killed in the Second World War and whose entire life plan had to be changed and adjusted. A well-known rector in an eastern city who never married and who suffered from recurring spells of mental depression, but whose sermons mailed to me each week made a profound difference in my own capacity to deal with life's problems. A tall lumberman skilled in mathematics but whose "typewriter couldn't spell." A gold medalist at making money, he nevertheless agonized over a mongoloid son. His agony caused him to open his eyes and his heart to the needs of other boys. He could always take time to teach a boy to use a saw or plane or to shoot a gun or drive a car or to fish. He and his wife poured thousands of dollars into those who needed glasses, dentures, operations, or college educations; wherever there was a need he did something about it.

Where does one stop in such a narrative? I could tell you of dozens who, like these, are the most loving and lovable people I know. And not one of them is an all-out gold medalist! Always a flaw or a hidden sorrow or some element that makes one come in second makes that friend an understanding person.

When someday I meet my Maker, as I expect to do, I do not think he will ask to see my gold medals. Rather, I think he will say, "What did you do with what you had? I'd like to see your silver medals or your bronze; in fact, I'd like to take a look at those times when you didn't win any medals at all." Coming in second—or even last with integrity and faith and compassion and self-giving—may ultimately be what it's all about.

Angry at Whom?
Fearful of What?

When a psychologist friend of mine told me that at the heart of every mental depression there was anger, I couldn't believe her. I had never been consciously aware before of being an angry person! And I had associated the emotion of depression with sadness, not anger. However, the more I thought of it the more I became convinced that she was right. Anger *is* responsible for lowered feeling and depression of spirit.

But, let me qualify. Being normal human beings we are so made that every one of us experiences anger as well as approval and affirmation. How could one appreciate sunshine without also experiencing darkness and gloom of rainy, wet weather? A certain amount of stress is good for us; in fact, the pull of stress within us challenges us to find new and different ways of dealing with problems and of solving them. A life completely placid and approving would stagnate from its very immobility. The heart of the matter is, however, the way in which we work out a balance in dealing with our anger as opposed to our approval.

My life as a child and a youth had no place for the expression of anger. I was taught that "he who is angry at his brother is in danger of hellfire." My parents were two generations older than I—I was born when they were forty-seven—and they were raised at a time when children should be seen and not heard. Woe be it if we dared criticize our parents! In that day you would be paddled soundly and sent to bed if you dared say, "I hate you!" And if something your parent did began to upset you emotionally, you just smiled sweetly and said nothing. Let me illustrate:

In the parsonage in which I grew up, there were only four years when I had a room to call my own. I had no sisters and four brothers. My parents had to have a bedroom; my brothers required two; my father had to appropriate one of the bedrooms for his study since our churches had none. In most of those rather large, two-story houses were both a living room and a parlor plus a dining room. But it did not occur to my parents to convert one of these rooms into a bedroom for me so that I might have some privacy.

In the house where my parents lived when I was away at college there was a sort of wide space at the top of the stair landing that was made into an improvised room. Here I slept when I returned home for Christmas and during summer vacation. Downstairs off the living room was a tiny room that my mother had made into a study for herself. I suggested that this become my bedroom during my stay at home, but my mother, having come from a family of nine, could not understand my need for privacy. Sleeplessness had never been a problem of hers!

My father, a true follower of John Wesley, arose at four in the morning to study and pray. However, the only way for him to get from his bedroom to the study was through my "bedroom." Being a light sleeper, I was awakened every morning as he made the transition. And I could seldom go back to sleep. Six o'clock was getting-up time at our house, and we all had to be present at breakfast.

Added to the injury of being awakened at four in the morning was the shaking of the wood stove and the building of the fire in the study adjoining my room and the praying aloud. There was a couch in Father's study, and it was placed against the wall that separated that room from mine. And so I lay awake, hearing those sometimes agonizing prayers while Father got things straightened out with the Lord for the day ensuing.

I am sure that to the day he died, my father never had any idea how my sleep pattern had been upset by his actions. Had I been raised in our day, I'd have simply demanded a room of my own or else planned to live elsewhere during the summer. And, by the same token, I am sure had I made it clear how deeply upset I was, both my parents would have moved toward correcting the problem. But, I was their good little girl; I had to win my Brownie points by pleasing them and asking no cut for myself. How very stupid! When I was growing up there was little known about self-realization or getting to know who you are. We were who we were and took what came our way, but we demanded little for ourselves.

I have forgiven my father long since. And my mother also. They didn't know what they were doing to me. But my nervous system hasn't forgiven them. My sleep pattern, along with the strain of the later breakdown, appears to have been totally disrupted. But the actual progress I have made since devoting myself to stress techniques is that I have separated the problem of sleeplessness from that of my religious faith. I lie awake because of my lifelong pattern of conditioning in sleeplessness and not because of lack of trust in God or Christian faith. I no longer feel guilty about the fact that I wake at two or three in the morning and can't go back to sleep. And because I do not feel guilty I can often go back to sleep after a time of deep breathing and meditation. Repeating Muriel's mantra (which I have quoted elsewhere), which has been used again and again in the stress classes I have taught, helps me as well.

I am in the process of training my will to accept the fact that my body does not need as much sleep as I had thought it did and that I can lie quietly, refusing to thrash around and keep moving my body, thus resting even if I am not asleep. But it takes constant training.

What can be said by way of encouragement and insight for those persons who long ago made a firm decision to let God into their lives but who have been thrown into a panic and a fearful abyss of darkness and lack of faith because of a sudden overload of stress? Years ago the late Dr. Georgia Harkness wrote a keenly perceptive book entitled *The Dark Night of the Soul*. If her experience has been yours, as well as mine, you know it is one of the most excruciatingly painful you can have. You have been a Christian all your life, and you have a very real faith. But an overload of stress coming your way in too brief a period of time throws you into a state of anxiety, and you cannot find God. You cannot even find the center of your being that has meant so much to you. You pray, but you pray in vain. God is out there somewhere, but you can't reach him. Part of the reason, of course, is physical. Your body, in responding to this new experience of *overstress* is really in *distress*.

Your heart feels as though it would pound right out of your chest; you have no appetite, and your weight drops perceptibly; your muscles are rigid and tense; your nerves are strung up as tightly as those of a violin about to be played; you literally feel as though you are about to jump out of your skin! You look in the mirror and almost do not recognize the agonized face you see; you become an insomniac and wonder where your old relaxed easiness and peace of mind have gone. Immediately you think you have the answer: "There's something terribly wrong with my faith. I am guilty of wrongdoing; I've 'missed the bus' and gone in the wrong direction, else I'd surely be able to find God. My faith must not have been all that great after all."

If, in your panic, you can accept the fact that you are dealing with stress symptoms and body symptoms you may never before have felt or experienced, rather than spiritual symptoms, you may be able to hang on until the light appears at the end of the tunnel. And if you can assure yourself that this is a situation that is physical and not a loss of faith, you'll come through. But most of us, while the panic persists and confusion overwhelms us, cannot do that. Morbid guilt sets in along with loss of meaning and a loss of the ability to allow our will to function. Cosmic loneliness lies all about us.

Now, while most of us do not go to the depths of despair when we experience an overload of stress, we do remain in the shallows of hopelessness and negativism. By ourselves we can't get out. It may take some psychiatric help, and it may take medication. But it may also take a bit of rethinking about the direction of our religious faith.

I did not discover until I was well along in years what

some of the Bible passages dealing with anger really mean. "Do not let the sun go down on your anger," "He who is angry with his brother," and others do not mean that you must keep from getting angry in the first place. But you must get that anger up and out before it festers deep inside you.

When you are feeling increasingly stressful and your anger is aroused, you can become objective rather than subjective, and the anger will lessen. One does not have to always give in to another; you must make your own thoughts and wishes clear. But you do not have to let your thoughts muddy the waters of your emotions in the process. Along with objectivity goes a sense of humor. Laughing at yourself is good medicine, indeed.

The mother-in-law of one of our minister friends had reached the age of 102. She lived near her daughter in a comfortable convalescent home. One day she heard a great commotion in the adjoining room. It seems the patient there was new and had been discovered to be an alcoholic who used the pretense of a doctor's appointment to go out and get her liquor supply. On learning that her "appointment" and the taxi had both been cancelled by the desk downstairs, she threw a mountain-sized tantrum, emptying all her dresser drawers onto the floor, slamming the doors, and breaking a vase on the opposite wall. The little centenarian went to the room, tapped on the door, and was allowed to enter. Calmly she explained that such action was not consistent with either the policy or the spirit of the home, that everyone there learned to live and let live. She ended her little heart-to-heart talk by saying to the self-centered newcomer, "And so now, my dear, I suggest you *cool* it!"

Wouldn't it be great to have such objectivity and self-worth at age 102!

In the study I have made of stress techniques, I have discovered that there is a strong relationship between the emotions of anger and fear. While anger lashes outward at the person you feel has been unjust toward you or the situation that has unfairly happened to you, fear is quite likely to go inward and be pointed at yourself. Of course there is healthy fear, and we all have it. It is what keeps us alert and provides a normal amount of stress that we need. But unhealthy, angry fear which has judgmentalism in its fiber is another thing to be reckoned with. It occurs when you question a judgment you have made or when you think you might have carried out the wrong course of action. It occurs also when your self-esteem is threatened. Your anger at yourself cries out, "Why on earth did I do such a stupid thing?" But your need to save face answers, "Don't admit it; don't acknowledge that you are such an insensitive, thoughtless person. You have spoken, and your word is worth something. Just let it go and make no effort to correct the error." But fear corrodes, and one fearful judgment made against oneself piles up upon another. Very soon one becomes afraid but is actually not quite sure just how to identify that fear. In the final devastating form, that angry fear within oneself grows into a dragon of fear of being afraid. And it becomes almost impossible to sort out the emotion step by step, correct it, and get rid of it.

If your anger is outward and aimed at another person or situation over which you have little or no control, you may explode beyond all provocation and, in the end, cut yourself off from further communication with the person or persons involved. This means that you have no chance of dealing constructively with any solution to the problem. If you can't get directly at the person or problem, you may find a scapegoat toward which to vent your venom. How many innocent children have received the cutting edge of a parent's anger aimed at the other parent and not at the child at all?

The church is constantly in this dilemma and receives the barbs and thrusts of persons who are actually angry at themselves but allow the church to become the scapegoat. "If only the youth program had done something for my son or daughter!" "If only so-and-so hadn't been the minister at that time!" But this same outward anger may go underground rather than explode outwardly. Perhaps you are too timid, because of early childhood conditioning, to actually bring your anger to the surface and allow it to be expressed verbally, and you cannot outwardly explode at all. The explosion takes place inwardly instead and is tucked away in the subconscious mind from which it emerges from time to time. It keeps being added to, and the whole mass ferments into either ulcers or a low-grade digestive upset that keeps recurring. Or you have migraine headaches and are given to periods of sullen brooding. Such anger, if not dealt with, can eventually erupt into chronic anxiety and neurosis.

There's an inner arrogance in us all—in some more than in others—that implies we are right. We may read more than others; we may be brighter and pick up more facts than another. And we may also lack a sound sense of self-worth. Our feeling of inner security and self-worth is shored up from time to time by giving forth these bits of knowledge so that we may get the reputation of thinking we know it all. When someone comments on our encyclopedic memory, we respond positively, for we know we are right. We remember the facts. But this feeling of rightness may invade the inner sanctum of our judgment, also, so that we may get the idea that our decisions and judgments are likewise always "right." And since no person can be perfect enough always to make the right decision, we bring down wrath or scorn from those closest to us when we are actually in error. This, in turn, brings inner fear, because we know we are wrong, but we have to feel we are right in order to maintain our inner security. Thus we are involved in a vicious circle from which we cannot extricate ourselves.

How does one deal with anger, either inner or outer anger, and resolve it before it becomes resentment? I am training myself to react in several different ways. First of all, using an insight from Recovery, I recognize that I am angry, and I start noting my body symptoms, for they are the first reactor to my emotional symptoms. I recognize the knot in the pit of my stomach, the fact that my voice is louder than usual, and that I begin to speak with more staccato and less softness. I feel the blood rush to my face, and my heart beats faster. I have an almost irresistible urge to prove my point, no matter how insignificant it is or how little the world is affected by whether I am actually right or wrong. I feel an invisible wall building up between myself and the person toward whom I am angry. My emotions tell me to "Keep still, say nothing," "You can't ever prove your point, anyway, why try?" "They are all older and wiser than you anyway," and on and on. But I know this is a replay of my little-girl emotions in a family surrounded by

67

persons older than I. Rather than clamming up or agreeing without full consent of my questioning nature or immediately running up a flag of truce, I try to ask some questions. Why do *you* feel as you do? How important to you is it that I agree? Your words make me uncomfortable, and I cannot get my mind to agree with what you say. Later on I try to put myself in the place of the one who has stirred my anger or in the situation that has provoked or devastated me and think of how I'd feel were I in the opposite role. This helps restore my perspective, and I see the situation in a wider context.

It is necessary, I think, to admit that everyone is ambivalent about anger and that it is possible to both love and hate. Our very humanity makes this truth possible. It is also possible to be very angry at the persons you love the most, but once admitted, the anger can be faced and usually resolved.

I can never forget an incident that happened well after I had begun to recover from the nervous and emotional breakdown that was mine in the 1940s. I could get only so far and no farther, it seemed. Outwardly my physical health had improved so that I was able to do household work and take care of my child as well as return to some of the church activities that my illness had caused me to drop. But there was still a cloud on my spirit, and I felt I was putting up a false front. The deep depression was not solved, and I knew it. I had noticed my husband's feet dragging somewhat, and that is most unusual for such a proverbial enthusiast. Also, my son's teacher at school sent a note home to us that our seven-year-old was refusing to play the games that the other children played. He just sat and watched them play. This, I knew, was a distress signal, and I was deeply troubled. All of a sudden, out of the despair of my depression, I cried out in great anger to God and said, "Okay, God, go ahead and send me to hell if you want to; but please, O please, don't let me drag my husband and son there with me." I amazed myself. But I cleared the atmosphere; and after that outburst, I slowly began to get better. With the lifting of my own depression came improvement to the spirits of the two I loved the most. I had dared to show my anger toward God! That would have been blasphemy in my growing-up years. Evidently I had been vastly angry and resentful toward God for, as I thought, promising me a baby and then withdrawing the promise. In actuality this was not true at all, but it was my personal interpretation. The expression of anger turned out to be a suggestion from God that I begin to take better care of the husband and child I already had.

Anger unrecognized can accumulate in the subconscious, and anger accumulated can become resentment. Resentment can then become depression. It is most necessary to find out exactly what you are angry about. It may take a long time to uncover, layer by layer, the accumulated angers. But it will be exceedingly worthwhile and necessary to your continuing mental health. It may so happen that our expectations for ourselves and those we love have been too high, and we must lower them, allowing our loved ones to have failures as well as successes. Likewise, we may have to lower our expectations for ourselves, especially if we are perfectionists and do not allow ourselves to be human or occasionally to fail.

We of the Christian faith have learned that confession to God with a prayer for forgiveness, then strength and courage and an acceptance of pardon, is our sovereign way of dealing with anger. Likewise, this is what Alcoholics Anonymous says the alcoholic must do. Realizing that he has harmed himself and possibly many people close to him in the pursuit of his obsession, he must make a strict moral inventory and seek to make amends whenever and wherever it is possible. He must confess his error and his sin to God and to one other. But, having taken this step he must forgive himself and go ahead. I believe the latter is what we all must do. If the anger or fear or anxiety is constant or too frequent to give us any peace of mind at all, we must learn to make amends when possible, seek forgiveness, and then learn that we are human and prone to mistakes. With too high expectations for ourselves, we must reduce the judgment against ourselves. We believe God will forgive us. But it is much more difficult to forgive ourselves. We are such perfectionists! And we hold impossible standards for ourselves. I can still hear my mother telling a friend, "Mary Ella can do anything she puts her mind to." And I really think she thought that. How mistaken she was! And what an impossible standard to present to any child. We Christians believe in God's grace and forgiveness. Let us learn to accept that forgiveness by dropping the judgment we hold toward others.

Anger can be dealt with but only if we have the will to keep eternally vigilant and work at it each time it appears. It is not a once-and-for-all matter of being solved. But the formula is a practical one and can solve your problem.

1. Recognize that you are angry and that it is natural to be so occasionally.
2. Locate your physical and emotional symptoms.

3. Bring your anger to the surface by admitting to the one who makes you angry that you are uncomfortable or threatened.
4. Put yourself in the other person's place, or see the situation through the eyes of the one on the other side of the fence.
5. Realize that it is normal to both love and hate. You are a human being.
6. Ask God's forgiveness and the forgiveness of the other person if your anger has harmed him or her.
7. Forgive yourself, lowering your expectations if you are a perfectionist.
8. Never allow anger to accumulate.
9. Ask God to keep your mind open to new possibilities in your relationships, to make fewer demands on those you love, to increase your love and decrease your judging, to do for your loved one what you are at present unable to do.

Is This Trip Necessary?

Anger and judgmentalism are twins, not identical but fraternal. Though unlike in appearance, they are almost always seen together. As typical brothers they fight between themselves. They both lay claim to being righteous, but the judgmental twin is inclined to hold grudges while his twin is more explosive but gets over his peeve faster. However, in the presence of others, each may tend to defend the other.

Actually, the matter of anger cannot be dealt with for any time at all without running headlong into the matter of judgment. Arguments within the family circle or at work among one's associates inevitably wind up with one party trying to prove I'm right and you're wrong, rather than objectively proving the relative merits or fallacies of the issue involved.

How often in discussions and panels over television I have seen one person just waiting for an opportunity to dive in and take over the disproving of another's arguments! This person doesn't even wait politely until the person speaking is through, nor does he or she listen to all the ramifications of what the opponent is saying.

The interrupter's eyes gleam, and he swoops into the center of the ring. And you know such a person is doing it not only to prove the argument but even more, to exclaim in triumph—though inaudibly—"I'm right! You're wrong!"

Two sisters whom I know, now in their sixties, share the same home. Likewise they share the running expenses of the household, such as the telephone bill. But there are points of difference between them amounting to a deadlock of temperament. One sister is convinced that she does a better job of answering the telephone, and so when it rings, she flies from wherever she happens to be working in the house and picks up the receiver. If the call happens to be for her sister, she will say with saccharine in her voice, "For you, Viola." Viola knows that no matter how quickly she moves or how much she may want to get to that phone first, her sister will always grab the receiver and be the first to answer. And the thorn of contention between them grows sharper with the passing of the years.

Now, what to do about the problem of judgmentalism? We all have it, some in marked degrees, and some in lesser degrees. I daresay if you were raised in a very strict, moralistic, rigid home, and if your family religion was of that sort, you have this problem of judgmentalism to a greater degree than the person who had a more accepting, tolerant home atmosphere. If your parents made a habit of enjoying their children and accepting their faults and failures, you may not be aware of having any judgmentalism in your nature. But I believe every one of us has a degree of this desire and the need to point the guilty finger at someone and proclaim, "I'm right! You're wrong!"

Again, you may be more widely read and better educated than other members of your family. And you may be better prepared from a standpoint of intellectual endowment. You have traveled more than they, and the basis of your contacts has been considerably wider than theirs. This makes it possible for you to be in possession of facts that they do not have. Or, a member of your family may have an even, analytical approach that enables him or her to confront an argument objectively, whereas you who know more facts about the ins and the outs of the problem cannot enter into an argument without becoming subjective and emotional. Therefore the other person, rather than you, always seems to come out ahead. You cannot win an argument; of that you are quite sure. But you have deep convictions and feel an urgency about letting them be known. A verbal clash ensues, but you are left always feeling you are the loser.

Finally, you may be a person who cares, and cares deeply, about your fellow beings. You have a very real sense of mission and a deep dedication to make the world a bit better for your having lived in it. However, it is difficult for you to take criticism and remain at all objective about it. You state your case, and you feel you have accomplished something worthwhile when along comes some member of your family or one of your associates who has far less dedication than you. And in a few well-aimed arguments, your well-intentioned dreams and plans are all knocked apart. You feel that perhaps what you started to do is not so important after all.

By your judgments you can ruin another person's self-esteem. You can likewise destroy your own self-esteem by beating yourself over the head and turning your judgments inward.

How shall I handle this judgmentalism toward another or toward myself? I have learned that when I become anxious about some criticism pointed at me or about my own critical attitude toward another and when I keep going over it in my mind without being able to feel comfortable about it or drop it, I first very quickly locate the physical symptoms I am experiencing. I have noted this technique before, and it is crucial. There is tenseness in my body, and I trace it to the muscles in my chest or to those going to my head from the right side of my neck. There is an empty feeling at the pit of my stomach or the lower abdomen, and I feel unusually tired, and my shoulders ache. Your symptoms may be entirely different from mine, given a similar situation. But symptoms we *do* have. I sense that I am angry, and I also sense that I am depressed, for there is little animation in my emotional reactions. I bring these symptoms into the foreground of my mind and examine them. "Why am I feeling upset? At whom? Myself? Another?" Then I try to see if there is judgmentalism on my part. Let us say that in the particular instance at hand, your irritant may be a grown daughter. You have been accustomed to controlling her behavior and letting her know when her philosophy conflicts with yours. Now she is in the driver's seat and isn't about to have you at the controls.

To control, or to manipulate, another human being, especially one you care deeply about, gives you a sense of security and power. It makes you feel greatly needed and increases your sense of self-importance. Control makes your loved one's reactions reasonably predictable, and you can be comfortable in the thought that the resulting behavior will be somewhat circumscribed. If your control seems not to be working, and you are feeling uncertain about its efficiency, you have certain methods of manipulation worked out whereby the control can be restored. Small children *need* to feel their lives have structure and that there is someone dependable at the controls. The most unhappy child, I have observed, is the least disciplined one, the one who feels that no one cares enough to set up barriers around and over which he or she may not pass. By your insistence as a parent that certain rules are laid out and adhered to, security is enhanced. But, suppose that child is now grown, and the parents can't detach themselves from the controls they have set up for his or her life? There is bound to be anger on the part of the youth as well as on the part of the parents. And judgmentalism also. The grown son or daughter appears to be a child, as caution is thrown to the winds and all the rules so strictly adhered to before now are broken. First the parents are shocked, for they are faced with an apparent stranger in the youth, once a child they knew so well—or thought they did. They confront their offspring with their wrath and their judgmentalism and find themselves trampled underfoot. The youth is wildly assertive and demands that the parents leave him alone to live his life as he wishes. And a stalemate of emotions ensues. What can be done?

Suppose you are such a parent. In this instance let us say the daughter to whom you related so closely has become a defiant stranger. Her behavior is notably obnoxious as she goes out of her way to break every rule you ever set up for her to obey. She laughs at your efforts at control and scorns your set of values. How can you deal with such a situation without losing your own mental health as well as the precious relationship that has been between you? First, locate your anger at her, then your anger at yourself. At what turn of the road did you hang on too tightly in your system of control? What methods of manipulation did you use in order to keep the relationship such a close one?

You have a right to express your anger and your frustration. And you need to do this verbally. You may say, "Your behavior alarms me. I am not only angry at your treatment of me, but I am angry at what you are doing to yourself. I hope you will seriously rethink your position." Having said this in no uncertain terms, you have stated your original response. The longer you keep mulling over in your mind what your offspring has done and is doing to you and to herself, the harder it will be to deal with the situation objectively. And if your imagination becomes embroiled, and you begin to fantasize about what she is doing and who she is with, you may be in for serious trouble. The facts in the case may become so entangled with your feelings about them that the reality of the situation cannot be viewed with any objectivity at all. It is well to recognize your mistakes in the relationship and to openly admit them, regardless of what the admission may do to your pride and self-esteem. Honesty is all-important. If you have a spiritual undergirding in your life, you will want to ask God's help in overcoming your shortcomings. This may not be done in a day or a week or a month or even a year. But it is necessary that you be determined to keep working at it. Regardless of how upset you may be, you and you alone can determine what your attitude toward the situation and toward your loved one will be. You may take a stubborn, negative, closed-minded attitude; or you may decide to take an open, positive stance with a willingness to change your mind at certain points that do not involve your deep moral convictions. You will tell yourself, "When asked I can make suggestions; but now that my child is of legal age I can no longer control her; she is responsible now for her own life, and we shall just have to wait to see whether the standards by which she has been raised will, in the long run, hold. She may still act like a child, but she is in reality a woman, and I must treat her with the respect due her age. I can no longer carry her load as well as my own. It is now hers to bear." You will become aware of the factors in her life that cause you to be judgmental, and you will forgive, realizing that thousands of parents face similar problems and learn to live with them. Of course, thousands of other parents deal with the problem of late adolescent revolt by saying, "Since you do not wish to live according to our standards, you may pack your clothes and find another place to live." But in the long run those parents are the losers. It is more important to maintain a relationship with those we love than it is to be right and then finally be proved wrong.

In talking with a friend of mine who has been active in Alanon and Alateen for years, I learned that these groups teach their people to deal with an alcoholic mate or parent or family member in much the same way. Where there is an alcoholic member of the family, the humiliation on the part of the other family members is great, and it is difficult to keep relating to a parent or a marriage partner or son or daughter who demonstrates such weakness as the compulsive habit of problem drinking. Though this goes on for years, and there appears to be no end in sight, one must remember that the whole story isn't written and may not be written for a long time. The most basic tenet of the Christian faith, I believe, is that persons can change by the grace of God. They change in the most miraculous ways! It happens every day; and it can happen to your loved one or mine.

At this point I want to make two or three ideas clear. I do think each of us has to make his or her own moral judgments, for I think there is a right way and a wrong way. I, personally, cannot accept the philosophy of permissive situational ethics. I think it is incumbent upon me to find out what is right and what is wrong for me and then to go about adhering to the rules required for such a course of action. However, I cannot make your value judgments by forcing on you my own. I am willing to make suggestions when asked; but I cannot control you or anyone else. In the final analysis no human being save Jesus the Christ can determine what my value judgments shall be. It is incumbent upon me to study Scriptures and learn what Jesus taught and how his life bore out his teachings. He got his directions from God, his Father. As a Christian I must finally do the same. I think it is crucial that we work for justice but that we leave the final judgment to God. The "last word" is never ours to speak; it is God's alone.

So many adults in our day are confused and at a loss. They have come to lean so heavily upon the advice of doctors, counselors, psychiatrists, and other specialists to make their value judgments for them, that their inability to formulate a philosophy of their own is appalling. They do not know what standards to set for their children or for themselves. They no longer listen for the inner voice, nor are they guided by the inner light so familiar in Quaker circles.

If one is in psychiatric analysis, it is all too possible to make the psychiatrist into God. This is a sobering thought, for if the counselor is clever but unscrupulous himself or herself, the patient's mind as well as his will may be damaged, while the psychiatrist or counselor reinforces his own power complex. I do not mean to assert that I disavow the services of psychiatrists—not at all! I've had the services of some of them myself, and two, especially, were of inestimable help. However, one psychiatrist to whom I was referred at the time of my breakdown told me to go into the bathroom three times a day and swear for a period of five minutes, for he felt sure that I was terribly repressed, and he thought this would give me freedom from that repression. I tried it once but found the whole experience a dismal failure. In the first place, I didn't know the words to use. And second, I came out of that bathroom with a deeper sense of guilt than I had had before, which was too much! Not until a consulting psychologist, who had grown up in a parsonage such as mine, helped me once again to pray, rather than learn to swear, did I find any sort of emotional release at all. And so with all my heart, if you need the services of a skilled psychiatrist, be careful to seek out the right one.

It is at this point that a spiritually-oriented sharing group of seekers within the church is all-important, both for insight and for support, not necessarily to supplement the psychiatrist or the psychotherapist but to follow up with the therapy of self-help in a Christian context.

These days, when I am tempted to be judgmental of

anyone or even of myself for a course of action, I ask myself a few questions.

Are you equipped with *all* the facts in the case?
Are you allowing judgment to crowd out the love you might be giving?
Are you too impatient to leave the final outcome to God?
Are you demanding to understand without being willing to love?
Is this trip really necessary?

To Err Is Human

The concept of forgiveness has all but dropped out of our thinking today. Many of us have been indoctrinated with the philosophy that seeks to have us understand our darker selves and come to terms with them by compromising our better selves. In other words, rather than bringing our behavior up to our standard of rightness and wrongness, we lower the standard to fit the behavior. At all odds we seek to be comfortable, whether or not that comfort violates our conscience that demands we do the right thing.

The Human Growth Potential Movement has emphasized again and again personal responsibility for oneself, and it has helped many people find the hidden talents within themselves. But often there is a noticeable lack of concern or personal responsibility *to* or *for* another. After all, if I and I alone am responsible for myself, then I assume every other person is responsible for his or her own life. But neither is, then, responsible for the other. However, as I understand it, the Christian faith emphasizes responsibility for my brother and sister. And that, traditionally, has meant anyone who needs my help.

Perhaps the problem is that we Christians have lost our sense of sin and wrongdoing. After all, if there is no clearly defined right or wrong, and if I'm okay, you're okay, why tell God or the other person you're *not* okay and seek forgiveness? And, if you assume complete control for your life and are entirely responsible for it, why assume you are responsible for anyone else? This, I think, is the real breakdown of many human growth movements: there is too much emphasis on self-development—intensely personal self-help—and too little on losing oneself in order to find oneself in service to others.

Too often the advice of some professional counselors is to "take a pill and keep still." I am indeed aware that there are illnesses that have as their origin biochemical imbalance. For them, medication is of the greatest importance. But a far greater number of miserably depressed or irrationally anxious persons have at the basis of their problem a guilt that is impossible to assuage. Guilt is the tangible evidence that there is sin mixed up in the malady. Forms of irresponsible behavior exact their inevitable price. Mentally disturbed persons need a clear, step-by-step method to move from their present condition toward health, toward community, toward usefulness. They need first to tell others the truth about themselves, as members of Alcoholics Anonymous do, and then to list the people they have harmed and set about to make amends wherever possible. Then, with growing health and increasing vitality replacing the crushing burden of guilt, they have an obligation to work with others who are seeking the same help. This will help ensure their own mental health.

I, personally, tend to feel that in our present Protestant

practice we rely much too heavily on group or public confession during the worship service itself and not enough on private confession to God. Both, I think, are necessary, but one type of confession need never supplant the other. Likewise, I have a strong feeling that confession has to be followed by doing something about it, else the confession lapses into idle words. This is a part of the great effectiveness of Alcoholics Anonymous, for its program is woven about making confession to "at least one other" and about changing one's thinking and one's life as direct restitution is made to the injured persons in the life of the alcoholic. Its philosophy is as sound as Christian conversion at its best, for after the process is gradually completed, the alcoholic is obliged to reach out and help another whose problem has been similar to his. And that help must be given all the remainder of his or her life. In fact, the alcoholic cannot stay out of trouble unless this outreach is practiced.

In this day of emphasis on psychology and counseling, many of us turn to the psychiatrist or analyst or marriage counselor or whatever other specialist we find most likely to meet our need and expect that person to be our mentor. After all, why bother God for forgiveness if the psychoanalyst can do the forgiving? We come away from the interview thinking a bit more clearly about what caused problems in the first place and why the symptoms still persist. But in a day or two the old burdens again lie heavily on our back, and we likely will not feel much different about ourselves or any more whole than we do now. Like the clock whose parts have all been carefully taken apart and laid on the table, we are torn apart and quite unable to put ourselves together again. Only God offers that salvation.

In the novel *Captain Newman, M.D.*, a patient who has become a compulsive alcoholic because of a guilty conscience submits to sodium-pentothal therapy. During the session he relives the awful moment he abandoned his best friend in a flaming plane that had been shot down over a steaming jungle in the South Pacific. He had run for safety and then remembered that his friend was burning to death in that plane. The whole tragic event had been so carefully concealed in his subconscious mind that he had never allowed himself to remember it. When the session was over, Captain Newman, the kindly physician—not only of men's bodies but also of their souls—reflects:

> For a moment you're that boy's God, and that's what I hate—at least a part of me hates it, the part that can be corrupted by power. . . . I hate myself for having to put his will at the mercy of mine—that's one reason why I don't use hypnosis . . . but after Pentothal they think they've had a wonderful sleep. Then *your* problems begin. How much do you tell them? How much do you hint? How fast can they take how much? When do you hold their hands? When do you get tough? Above all, what's RIGHT? *What's RIGHT for the rest of their whole lives?* And who has the right to decide? Do *I* set boundaries for guilt, or administer dosages of pain or penance? Hell! I'm a doctor—that's all. But I am the one who has to stand between his sanity and the merciless forces—panic, guilt, conscience, that put him there. (Rosten, p. 126)

Again, I say, we lay too much of a burden on the shoulders of the analyst or on the professional psychologist who is our counselor. This person may help us be able to forgive the one who wronged us or possibly to forgive ourselves, even though our nervous system scarcely ever forgives us for the damage we have allowed it to suffer. But to really *feel* forgiven—there's the rub! In the final analysis, only that Power greater than our own, God, our Creator and Redeemer, can bring about complete forgiveness.

In *Life Together,* the late Dietrich Bonhoeffer wrote:

> In confession the break-through to community takes place. Sin demands to have a man by himself. It withdraws him from the community. The more isolated he is the more destructive will be the power of sin over him, and the more deeply he becomes involved in it, the more disastrous is his isolation. Sin wants to remain unknown. It shuns the light. In the darkness of the unexpressed it poisons the whole being of a person. This can happen even in the midst of a pious community. In confession the light of the gospel breaks into the darkness and seclusion of the heart. The sin must be brought into the light. The unexpressed must be openly spoken and acknowledged. All that is secret and hidden is made manifest. It is a hard struggle until the sin is openly admitted. But God breaks gates of brass and bars of iron. ([New York: Harper & Brothers, 1954], p. 19)

Why is it so difficult for us to forgive one another? Why cannot children forgive their parents? Why cannot parents forgive their children? Why cannot husbands and wives forgive each other? Why do people hold such deep-seated resentment against the church?

Overemphasis on some aspects of psychology for several decades has thrown a dark blanket of guilt about the shoulders of thousands of parents who have tried especially hard to be good parents to their children. But because their children have turned away from the old values and standards that they were taught as children and youths, the parents now feel they have completely failed in their parenting. Henry T. Close, a chaplain in Atlanta who has worked with many such parents, has written one of the most penetrating articles I have seen on the subject of forgiveness, "On Parenting."

There is no question but that your parents failed you as parents. All parents fail their children, and yours are no exception. No parent is ever adequate for the job of being a parent, and there is no way not to fail at it. No parent ever has enough love, or wisdom, or maturity, or whatever. No parent ever succeeds.

This means that part of your task—like that of every other person—is to supplement what your parents have given you, to find other sources of parenting. You need more mothering than your mother could give you, more fathering than your father had to offer, more brothering and sistering than you got from your siblings.

The problem is complicated by the demands our society makes on parents to be good parents. They are supposed to be 100% adequate, and it is a terrible mistake if they are not. If they are successful, their children will reward them with devoted love, obedience, and success; if they are not, their children will turn out to be unloving, disobedient, and unsuccessful. This is the prevailing conviction of our society. But when parents buy this notion, they put themselves in an impossible position. They try first to be 100% adequate. And then, when they inevitably fail at this, they try to appear 100% adequate. In either case, they cling to you, demanding that you get all your parenting from them, thus reassure them that they have been good parents. They may also demand that you be loving, obedient, and successful, since this would be living proof of their success as parents. Such parental concern about children's 'failures' can be understood in part as an attempt to force the children to succeed, and thus reassure the parents that they have been good parents. They thus find it difficult to let you grow up—that is, to find other sources of parenting. This means that you will have to grow up in spite of them rather than wait for their permission. They will not make it easy for you, and you must do it on your own.

To grow up, it is necessary to forgive your parents. But you must forgive them for your sake, not theirs. Their self-forgiveness is up to them, not you, and they cannot afford to wait for you to forgive them any more than you can afford to wait for them to forgive you. When you do not forgive them, it means that you are still expecting all your parenting from them. You are clinging to them in the hope that if you can make them feel guilty enough, they will finally come through with enough parenting. But this is impossible, and in order to be really free to find other parenting, you must forgive.

I hope you will not be embarrassed at your need for parenting, and that you will be humble enough and determined enough to find effective ways of getting it. (*Voices: The Art and Science of Psychotherapy*, 4 [Spring, 1968])

At the present time I know quite well three mothers left widowed to raise their children, who are feeling very alone and desolate because of neglect by their now grown children. When the husband died, each woman rose to the task of being both father and mother to the children, and all went surprisingly well. But now that the last child has left home or is about to leave, there is a sense of ambivalence, a doubt as to the worth of their mothering and a feeling of rejection and desertion. In the case of all three families, one or more of the children has turned away from the church of the parents. And the mothers feel a bit bitter about the fact that the leadership of the church was not strong enough to hold youths, thus allowing them to slip away from its worship services and its fellowship.

Here I want to quote from the column "Himself" by the well-known and somewhat controversial Charles McCabe of the *San Francisco Chronicle*. After quoting statistics telling of the decline of membership and attendance within the church, he reveals that after years of alienation from the Catholic Church, he has now become a regular attendant and an occasional communicant.

> If I am honest with myself, I have to admit that I came back to the Church I was born into for no very admirable reason. I came back because I felt better sitting in a church pew, witnessing the Sacrifice of the Mass, and listening to the comfortable platitudes of the preacher.
>
> The Church is not called Mother Church for nothing. A break with it is as significant and upsetting an experience as a bitter and lifetime quarrel with a mother or a father. There is the same vague anxiety, which never seems to go away. There is the sense of being a split person. There is, above all, a sense of the loss of innocence.
>
> A man cannot be whole unless he has composed his quarrels with those who gave him being. It is hardly an inconsistency that I returned to the Catholic fold shortly after my mother died. I had more or less composed my ancient quarrel with her before her death. Her death completed the peace-making process. Her death also made it clear to me that the other quarrel, so closely related to my quarrel with her, must be composed if I were to regain myself.

In my own case I have found it more difficult to forgive myself than to forgive those who caused me mental or emotional grief. I suppose this is for the very reason that I have a bit of a God complex and find it almost impossible to accept failure. I've had to accept a lot of it, but the acceptance does not come easily as I have noted already. For years I could not forgive my father, most especially, for disturbing my sleep and causing me to be an inveterate insomniac. I preferred to suffer in silence rather than risk his anger and ill will. And so, if anyone is at fault, I should admit it rather than blaming him. Alas, I never got a chance to tell him before he died. Likewise, I could not for years forgive myself for not recognizing certain symptoms involved in the sudden death of our little son David Kent. I flagellated myself unendingly for not having taken better care of him, knowing full well all the time that I was not a diagnostician nor a nurse but only a human being with limited knowledge and insight. The God complex again. I know my Father God forgives me as I know my loved ones do. And at last I have made peace with myself about it. But in both these as well as other traumatic incidents in my life, my nervous system bears the scars and won't forgive. This I can do nothing about. What is done is done. I do know, however, that suffering and grief make me more compassionate in understanding others who go through the Valley of the Shadow. And I know that I need never go through such experiences completely alone. God is with me.

Jesus said much about the necessity of forgiveness. And if we are to be his followers and experience the companionship of his living presence, we too must forgive and seek forgiveness when we have erred. It was not just a passing whim when Jesus told the story of the prodigal son, or when he said one must forgive not once or even seven times but rather seventy times seven—endlessly. He also told his disciples that if they were about to lay their sacrificial gifts on the altar of the temple but on the way suddenly remembered that they had had a quarrel with someone dear to them, they should leave and make peace with the person at odds with them and then come and make their offering to the Most High. It is not enough to excuse or overlook. We must go all the way. We must forgive.

Finally, one of the most difficult of all things to do, or so I think, is to forgive the person (and to keep forgiving) who does not even seem to know he or she is in need of forgiveness. For that person, forgiveness is never asked and its need never acknowledged. But you realize that great harm has been done and that if you are to live with that person as a friend, and more particularly with yourself, you must forgive and keep forgiving. This gets into the realm of divine forgiveness. It is something akin to the way Jesus must have felt when he prayed from the cross, "Father, forgive them, for they know not what they do."

Certainly sometime, if not in our time, then in God's own time, there will come understanding, and we shall know why we do some of the things we do and why we stand so desperately in need of forgiveness. But until that time, we must forgive, not seven times but seventy times seven. Endlessly.

To Care and Not to Care

To control stress is to match outer stress with one's own internal stability. If you are a rigid person, you are likely to become immobilized by a heavy load of outer stress. On the contrary, if you can endure sudden change and become more elastic, more open, more willing to listen to the viewpoint of another, you may be able to bend like the character pine. By being able to slowly bend you will gradually be able to live with your inner stress in the midst of outer stress.

A concept that I learned in Recovery is appropriate here. There is such an idea as outer and inner environment to be incorporated in one's thinking. In this book I have mentioned inner and outer stress; but that stress must have some realm in which to work or to be contained. This we recognize as environment.

That which goes to make up my physical body and its functions might be termed inner environment. This is the aggregate of my physical being, including the functions of my mind—both conscious and subconscious. It includes my will, my power to reason and dream, to plan, to appreciate beauty, to relate to other human beings. It is that which I know to be my personality, that which makes me unique and which distinguishes me from any other person and makes me different from an animal. It is that which I call *myself*.

That which lies outside myself is my outer environment and includes my husband and my son who is no longer a part of our household but still a very important part of our lives and our thinking. It includes my friends here and around the world and all the people whose lives touch mine in any way. It includes my neighborhood and its noisy motorcycles and its beautiful view of the bay, and it sometimes includes the noise of the planes as they swoop over our hill when the wind is in one certain direction. It includes our community and those who surround it in ever-widening circles. It includes the weather, the nation, the earth on which I live. And if it is proved that there is life on one of the other planets, it will include the people and environment there. Everything that is outside this being that I call myself becomes a part of my outer environment.

Now, I am responsible *to* all these persons and to the pertinent factors that affect my life in one way or another. But I cannot be responsible *for* them. Jesus taught that all persons whose life touches mine are my brothers and sisters, and I am responsible to them. I may try to influence them in whatever constructive way possible; I am called to have goodwill toward them and to love them, to help whenever possible, never wishing them ill. But they themselves must be responsible for their lives as I am responsible for mine. Quite naturally, I am responsible for my children until they are old enough to assume more and more responsibility for themselves. When they are grown I am no longer responsible *for* them but rather *to* them. As a Christian, I am responsible to God, my Father, who cares deeply whether I make my life a beautiful and helpful one for him. And with his help I am responsible to him for my own life and behavior.

I want to reiterate a fact that I have learned. In time of crisis I am much more afraid of my body and emotional symptoms than of the actual crisis itself. I have discovered that most people handle sudden crises rather well. When death comes to our loved ones or when divorce has to be lived through, or any of several such personal crises, we find ourselves performing and enduring better than we had expected. But handling the reaction of our body to that emergency may present a different and more frightening problem. For example, how often have I turned in upon myself and thought, "You are a coward!" when all the time my nervous system was reacting to the beating it had taken. I the person, Mary Ella Stuart, who had actually made a rather courageous reaction to the outer stress that had come my way, was not really being cowardly at all. In fact, I had responded well under duress.

Did you ever have your knees buckle under you *after* a terrifying experience rather than during the performance? Six weeks after I received my first driver's license (at age thirty-five) I crashed into the rear end of a car whose driver made no turn signal to let me know she was pulling to the curb. Being given a citation I had to appear in court to defend myself. Inwardly I was frightened but was outwardly cool. I knew that I had been within the limits of the law and that the other driver had failed to signal a stop. The judge asked me to describe the accident, which I did. Then he asked the officer who had written out the citation to give his story of the accident. He related, among other things, that I had been driving rather closely behind. But when the judge asked about the signal to stop, he turned to me and said, "Did she give you a signal that she was stopping?" I replied, "No, Your Honor, she did not." And he said quickly, "Case dismissed." I walked very matter-of-factly out of the courtroom, but when I got to the long flight of steps, my heart pounded and my knees buckled so that I had to hang on to the handrail while walking down the steps. This is a typical reaction, I have discovered. We fear our body sensations more than we actually fear the outer environment factor that is disturbing us.

In dealing with inner or outer environment I must first determine the extent of my responsibility and that for which I can be held accountable. It is astounding to discover how many people have not as yet fully assumed responsibility for their personal lives. The old dependencies and images of childhood linger on and seem almost impossible to shake. Or, an earthshaking and long overdue or postponed adolescent revolt takes place, shattering your inner environment and the control of your well-organized life much as a tornado that tears up the houses and trees and ground in its path, leaving a shambles of what had been a well-run village. Likewise, this postponed adolescent revolt adversely affects your parents or your mate or your children—those closest to you—leaving them devastated by the change that has come over you. You may manage to survive, finding that you aren't independent or responsible for your own life after all. Your newfound freedom is simply an exchange of one dependence for another. Whereas you were once almost totally dependent upon a parent, you now find yourself to be almost as dependent upon a husband or wife or upon a grown son or daughter or upon a close friend. Or your dependence may be on having plenty of money or prestige or any of a hundred different factors in your new life. You may become dependent upon promiscuous sex outside of marriage or upon "swinging" and sharing your sex life with many couples. You may depend upon being surrounded by people and be unable to face solitude. The dependencies are innumerable. Often one is able to find a bit of ground of one's own on which to stand. But a certain degree of damage has been done to both inner and outer environments in the process of finding that independence.

It is a great day when one can declare with the whole of the inner being, "I am responsible for my life. I am a creature who has the power of choice. I shall no longer blame circumstances of my life, my parents, my adverse combination of genes, or my outer environment for who I am or what I am, and I intend to make my life worth living." It is a greater moment still, I believe, if one can say in truth, "I am in tune with the rhythm of the universe. I have committed my whole self to a Power greater than my own so that when my very humanity makes mistakes inevitable, I can know that Someone is helping me carry the load of it. Thus, while I seem to be alone in the world, I am actually never alone!" In my experience, no person who has gone to pieces, lost his or her self-esteem, and then found a firm place on which to stand did so without being loved greatly by someone—someone who had enough faith and confidence in that person to help in his or her recovering a sense of worth as a human being.

Some persons are irresponsible, have always been that

way, and most likely always will be that way. Since the day they were born—or so it seems—other people have had to carry their burdens, clean up after them, make excuses for them, and become surrogate parents in their behalf. These persons never comprehended the biblical concept of being their brother's (or sister's) keeper and likely never will. They have a way of being unable to be counted on when they are needed. They remind one of the little boy who was five, and his girl, four. He told his mother that they were going to get married. She gave some thought to what he had said and thinking she would handle his suggestion adroitly said:

"It costs a lot to get married."

"I get forty cents a week, and she gets twenty-five. We can live on that."

"It takes a place to live. What will you do about that?"

"She has a dollhouse. We are both small; it's big enough for us."

Then she realized she must really break through. "Couples have babies, and this is a big responsibility. What will you do about this?"

"If she lays any eggs, we will break 'em."

In almost every family today there are the irresponsible ones who live together, outside the marriage vows, not too much more grown-up than these two children, "playing house." Or so it appears to me.

On the other hand, there are persons who care and care deeply. They always concern themselves with the problems their friends, relatives, and neighbors face, and they try to help shoulder the load along with their own already heavy load. Their caring is deep and genuine, but they care *too* much. Sometimes this excessive sense of responsibility comes from one's own childhood. If you were the oldest child and had to take care of younger siblings in the family, it is quite likely you may now feel overloaded with responsibility. If you were in the middle, you may have actually felt you were neither fish nor fowl and that no one particularly needed you. It didn't matter much if you did or did not help carry responsibility. And if you were the youngest child, others may have felt responsible for you rather than your feeling so for them.

Because of my profound early sense of responsibility, there grew within me a feeling that things would totally collapse if I were not there to hold them together. And I have never quite been able to get rid of that albatross about my neck.

This overresponsibility I have termed the "Atlas complex." A poem that is in my scrapbook illustrates the point. I do not know the author:

Atlas has many aides; my strength is small,
And when I offered it, "My child," he said,
"I have more helpers than I want or need—
This task was mine since time began. If all
Stand here with me, and sweat, and groan, and bleed,
Who shall see the glory overhead?"

If you are the kind of person who is up tight because you feel a sort of responsibility for bringing the sun up in the morning and putting it away at night, if you think God needs your help in determining the weather, and you must apologize to your friends because it isn't as beautiful and warm for their visit as you had hoped, if you feel a terrible burden for the coming election and for the destiny of the nations that you cannot influence, and if you feel you must control the life-style and ultimate destiny of your grown-up son or daughter, have another thought and remember that poem.

The poem represents, does it not, the idea of outer stress bearing in on inner stress? But if the inner stress is in control, there is tranquility and a certain detachment that controls inner stress. Stress and tranquility—there's a paradox in that thought. How can you have both at the same time? How can you be all keyed up for action and serene and calm at the same time? How can you care deeply and yet not care?

Well, for one thing, you can let go your favorite security blanket. Several years ago I was talking with a psychiatrist friend of mine in another state and telling him about our Anx Anon group which was such a real part of my life in the early sixties. One of those young matrons, after I had moved away and the meeting of the group had discontinued, committed suicide. Too much stress because of various outer environment factors had borne in upon her, and she had taken that fatal dose of barbiturates that stole away her life. I was very upset about the situation: she had been a Phi Beta Kappa from Stanford, wrote delightful children's stories, and was one of the best-read persons I have ever known. I not only admired her, I loved her dearly. However, during the course of our meetings, she would never promise the others of us in the group that at some time or another the way out of her problem might not be suicide if things got too bad. I knew all too well that life doesn't work that way, for I had been on the verge of psychosis and had attempted that escape myself. I promised God that never again, so long as I lived, would I resort to such means for ending the life he had given me. I knew if she would only do the same, she'd fight to live on *any* terms. And in the struggle she would find herself. But she always evaded the issue and would not make the promise. I asked my psychiatrist friend about the validity of trying to get such a promise from her. And I shall never forget his response. He rose from his chair, and with fire in his Irish blue eyes, he shouted, "That's just the problem! We keep hanging onto our security blankets! We know they aren't going to get us anywhere, but we can't bear to let go of them. I sometimes think that the last patient that steps over that threshold, hanging onto a security blanket, is going to get the hell knocked out of him and be kicked all the way to the street, just for hanging onto a security blanket!"

I was amazed at his fiery outburst and asked in a very little voice, "What is *my* security blanket?" And he replied not too gently, "Your great big outsized sense of responsibility!" Since that time I have worked away at this Atlas complex of mine, and it has lessened. Again and again I say to myself when I am perturbed about something a loved one does, "That's not my problem. I have enough to do just keeping Mary Ella Stuart in line to keep me busy for the remainder of my days." This sense of responsibility lies at the heart of thousands of anxiety neuroses. We have such a need to be needed, don't we?

First, it is essential that we find out who we are and what makes us tick. As for me, I am a person who has an 80 hp drive in a chassis that has about a 40 hp motor. Every family has its familial health problems, and those of my family's appear to be an inherent weakness in the central nervous system. Multiple sclerosis, muscular dystrophy, Parkinson's disease, and nervous breakdown have felled some of us and threaten others. This is my physical heritage of weakness along with some great physical strengths. But I need always to remind myself, "O woman, thou art mortal!" Don't ever think you are God. At any time you could fall on your face, and don't forget it! At the same time I realize that some of the greatest people have struggled with some of the frailest physical bodies and have brought forth beauty out of their lives in spite of it. And this I purpose to do, God being my helper! The power of choice is mine.

The essential person I am cannot stand to live with a poor sport or a grouch, and since in the final analysis I have to live with myself, I am determined not to be a whiner, even if I have to be a clown to prove it. I don't particularly enjoy fearful, dependent, helpless people; so I must keep from being that way myself. I must remain as independent as is possible without flaunting my precious freedom as a person, or as a woman either. I must make as many of my own decisions as possible, and I must have moments when I can completely endorse myself as a person for what I have done and for who I am. I have to like me! I admire persons with both a deep faith and a sense of humor; so that's what I must cultivate in myself. I must keep certain priorities for my life in mind, and I must care deeply about people and about life itself but not make a desecration of that caring.

Much of this chapter has been about dealing with inner stress more than with outer stress, for if you can deal with what's inside you, you can take the buffeting from outer environment and bend without breaking. Realizing that I am, in fact, more afraid of my inner feelings and sensations than of what may come at me

101

from the outside also helps. Each stress I handle well makes me know that the next one will not likely completely destroy me. Realizing that, having the body and temperament I have, I shall likely always have quite a lot of discomfort to bear, while not a comforting thought, is facing the truth about myself and not kidding myself about what I am up against. Having experienced great distress I know that this, too, shall pass away, if I wait long enough and trust God's unfailing grace. Knowing that no matter how low my physical and nervous vitality may be at the moment or how weak my will may be this hour, I realize I always have the power of choice before me. God says, "Thou mayest, if thou wilt." I know that I simply have no right to say, "I just couldn't make myself do it." Rather, what I am saying in the weak moment is, "I really don't care to do it." In other words, I am responsible for me, and I am not just a piece of driftwood tossed hither and yon by the waves.

In my mind's eye I have a picture of my outer and inner environment. My inner environment is a tiny island surrounded by a moat. In a cottage on this island I live. I am connected to the outside world by a drawbridge that is open much of the time to allow the persons on the other side of it to get to me, and I to them. But it is possible for me, if I choose, to pull up the drawbridge and not allow someone to cross. The persons closest to my drawbridge are the ones of my family and those with whom I work and for whom I am at least partially responsible. And they are the ones with greatest access to my island and to my bridge. But there are times when, as much as I love them, I will not let them cross over that bridge to invade my sanctuary. Only God is there perpetually, as he is everywhere.

I must deal with my own problems, with those of my husband, and with some of the problems of others who mean much to me and who, in turn, bring richness to my own life. But I can go so far and no farther. Beyond a certain point I must know that the problem is theirs and not mine. Leaving them in "outer environment" means "You take care of them, God—I've gone about as far as I can."

If children are very young, they must have almost constant access to the parent and to his or her little island. I the parent am responsible for their very existence for a time—the first few years of life. I must see to it that they eat balanced meals, have the shelter of a loving home, are provided comfortable clothing, meet other children with whom to play, have a place of their own to which they can go and not be disturbed or their privacy not be invaded. All these and more! But I cannot be responsible for their happiness. This they must find themselves. When they are grown I may occasionally offer help or suggestions. But I cannot control. I'd better not try controlling my husband either. It just doesn't work. I have to be the person in control of my own life. And the only way I have ever found to successfully exercise this control is to turn over the controls to my Father, God. So long as I know I am doing his will, I can be his person and, thus, myself.

The Energy Crisis

Almost every person who is doing any serious thinking today knows about the energy crisis. It looms like a specter, not only in our country but in most countries of the world. But, for the most part we are not inclined to do much about change. In the first place we are not all that convinced that immediate action is mandatory. We have had the cry of "wolf, wolf" again and again from our government in many different areas, and we are at a loss to know how great the emergency is. It is like the atomic bomb and the reports about how widespread its production is. Because we cannot see it or touch it or feel it, we do not realize its deadly power. After all, it has never as yet been turned to our own destruction.

One serious look at the problem of energy in our outer environment allows us to see that the problem lies not only in our lack of credibility but also in our ineptitude as a nation in dealing with the situation. Because we cannot see far enough ahead to project what will happen, we refuse to set ourselves as a people to spend the necessary funds and the scientific research and engineering necessary to correct the problem.

The problem is not only with lack of energy, we are told. It is with the source of supply itself. Too little food for too many people depletes the energy of the masses. And inability to substitute solar energy and atomic energy for oil and natural gas makes it impossible to keep warm enough in winter or cool enough in summer. Unless we can learn, and learn soon, to go to the source of this energy and discover how to appropriate its power, we shall be without the vital energy that makes our corporate life possible. And unless we can decide to spend the necessary funds whereby salt can economically be taken from sea water to make it available for raising crops and for drinking, we are told by scientists, we shall soon face crisis in this vital area of need.

Corporate lack of energy, as great as that problem is, is not our number-one enemy to be conquered. Our very greatest lack is the energy crisis within each of us as individuals. Too many people rise every morning feeling unrested, inadequate for the work of the day, having been kept awake by the noisy thoughtlessness of neighbors in too close proximity or by an uneasy conscience that will not let them rest in assurance that "God's in his heaven and all's right with the world." We skim through that which has to be done immediately but never seem to complete to our own satisfaction the tasks to be done before our steam runs out. Our list of complaints is unending. Our roots are too shallow and planted in the thin "now" of existence. We have forgotten the precious heritage of our history as a religious people who relied upon God for the strength that we ourselves could not generate; and we are very puzzled when we contemplate our lives' going on beyond this short span of years into still another life.

We are a people run down, confused, and, like an orchestra that has played too long without a pause, rather badly out of tune. But before a great orchestra ever becomes one voice with a majesty of power in its performance, its members must practice and practice, listening for the slightest deviation in pitch or time, which might mar the total theme being presented. Its members are led by the conductor, who can determine the end result and make the music sound as he wants it to sound. To become a member of a symphony orchestra the individual player must expend hours of discipline and study, as well as practice, day after day, week after week, year after year as a minimum requirement. And if you are that player who is so fortunate as to be selected, you must practice in much the same way as long as you remain a performer. Training in listening and bending one's own interpretation to that of the director is required. You are not playing solo; you are playing in an ensemble, and your conductor sensitively shapes that coherent whole.

However, life is so constructed that one cannot constantly give energy from oneself without taking in a given amount of energy in return. Like the beating of the heart with its diastolic and systolic rhythm, so is all life. The very busiest person has to learn, early in his or her career, to compensate for the output of emotions. And when the only process one has ever known is the will process, this technique often breaks down.

The dull, rather monotonous, and very rigid routine through which we were put in one Human Growth group that I attended would not have been one I'd have elected to expose myself to, had the need not been great. But as with so many persons experiencing emotional trauma, it was either that or chaos. And so, in the nine months I spent with that group I learned much about disciplined training of the will. Certainly power came to me through the effort.

My son has shared with me some lines of poetry by C. Day-Lewis, which sum up I think this sense of hoping that if one just practices an act of will, over and over, something dramatic will happen:

and though my todays are
Repetitive, dull, disjointed,
I must continue to practice them over and over
Like a five-finger exercise,
Hoping my hands at last will suddenly flower with
Passion, and harmonize.
(*Collected Poems of C. Day-Lewis* [London: Jonathan Cape with the Hogarth Press, 1954], p. 278)

But this gaunt hope is not enough, is it? For me, at least, it has become apparent that power had to come from somewhere outside of myself, or it would not come at all. And it had to come by something beyond the mere technique of self-training of the will.

I recall one evening when in a meeting of the group that I attended, one of our members gave an example of a trip he and his two teen-aged daughters made to a midwestern state. None of the three had traveled by plane before, and our member had never been used to planning schedules or making arrangements that the seasoned traveler learns to do by rote. He said that he kept waking up during the night at fifteen-minute intervals, expecting the alarm to sound, and feeling it must be time to get up and dress in order to be ready for the arrival of the taxi that was to take the three to the airport. He was afraid to take medication for fear he'd fail to hear the alarm; so he lay awake much of the night. Again and again he did the necessary "spotting" that he had been taught in the group to do. But nothing happened. He did not turn over and peacefully go to sleep but rather found himself more awake than before. He cried out to the group, "What do you do when the only technique you know completely fails?"

Yes, what *do* you do? This is the typical feeling of the neurasthenic: "There ought to be a way of handling this problem, but what?"

We of the Christian faith know that there is a point at which one has to stop trying and simply wait for God to do something. You've played your last card, and now it is his move. If you try beyond this point, the harder you try, the more tangled you become in your own ball of emotional yarn.

People of our day are hearing more and more about yoga, about transcendental meditation, about relaxation techniques. It appears to me that in the past several decades the church has failed to stress its own unique meditative techniques. The practice of sharing experiences by testimony and mutual prayer has all but gone out of vogue. Instead, these techniques have been turned over largely to the secular agencies. They must be painfully relearned, I believe, if the church is to inwardly strengthen its people.

At this point I want to say that what I have heard of transcendental meditation is on the very positive side and not the negative, likewise with yoga techniques. I have several friends trained for years in Christian techniques, practicing Christians themselves, who have also experienced TM and yoga. They have gained much from both by way of relaxation.

These are fields that I myself should like sometime to explore. For I feel that in the past our methods of praying have been too much on the active side and not enough on the passive. We have done too much talking to God and too little listening. And we have expected results that are within the scope of our understanding rather than the seemingly impossible, which God sometimes does for us despite our asking. I think most of the Human Growth techniques can be adjusted and translated into Christian terms. The chief problem comes, I believe, when the person involved has no religious background whatsoever.

One member of the group to which I referred confided to me that he had been in the group for almost fifteen years and that it was his "church." I concede that it does serve as a group fellowship and might, as in his case, be very beneficial. However, its technique is the self-centered training of the will with no moral mandate, no obligation to humankind, no feeling at all that I am my brother's keeper. Thus it can result in a self-contained and sometimes stagnant pool rather than a fresh-running stream fed at its source by a spring that never dries up and runs in a swelling tide out to mingle with the ocean.

Years ago I read a story that has remained with me vividly through the years. It was written by a woman who spent the first fifteen years of her life in a horizontal position, for she had a curvature of the spine, and doctors knew of no other way to treat the malformation. During the years when she began to be able to walk and take on a life other than that of complete invalidism, she underwent a breakdown. In her case it was agoraphobia, though she did not know by what name to call the malady. For so long she had remained in one position and was so confined within the limits of her own home and her adoring family that when she began to explore the outside world, she gave way to panic. The wide-open spaces filled her with an unknown phobic terror of the concepts of timelessness and endlessness. But all on her own she found a way to outwit the creeping paralysis of fear that overwhelmed her with panic. She would fix her eyes upon some object—a flower, a tree, or a piece of furniture—anything near her or within her vision. Laboriously she would go over every minute detail of its beauty: the way in which it was put together, the lines and formations of wood, the petals of a flower, the details of a table or a chair. If it had color, she would drink in the beauty of it and wonder what combination of colors had gone into its makeup. Eventually her confusion would vanish, and her world would be familiar again and all one piece. Through this process she discovered God and communicated with him, for her family was not a religious family, and prayer was not natural to her. And her thankfulness began to know no end. She at least was vertical, could walk, and could participate in life as did her family members. And her phobias gradually left her.

I recall that at the close of her book she mentioned "the dark age" we seemed to be entering. (That was thirty years ago.) She said she thought this was happening because we, the inhabitants of this beautiful earth, had forgotten that we had come from we knew not where and were going to we knew not where but in the process had forgotten that we were guests on this earth, very rude guests who had forgotten to thank the Creator who made us for the privilege of living here. She said we had grown "suicidally clever" in our belief that we "had all the answers" and had forgotten our manners. And she added that if we were all destroyed and if in some distant future a new breed of people were allowed to inhabit this sphere, it would be a simple one, who bowed down each day as the flower bows to the sun and the rain, acknowledging a great dependence upon its Creator, just for the privilege of being alive.

This, I believe, is what prayer is: first, appreciation, acknowledgment of our dependence upon a Power greater than our own, a still waiting for our lives to be filled with that Power, and a going forth with renewed spirit to do whatever we are directed by that Power to do and to be.

In the classes that I have been teaching, we always begin with a period of relaxation with somewhat the same technique as this little hunchback discovered. And after the lesson and the sharing on the part of the members of the group of some trivial situation in order to gain insight into the greater problem that is ours, we close with Muriel's mantra.

Let me tell you about Muriel. She is a dear friend who has spent much of her life taking care of a son who from his first year on earth was a victim of cystic fibrosis. This disease is caused by a dysfunction of the pancreas causing serious digestive disorder. Along with this malfunction, the lungs are affected and breathing is made difficult and finally impossible. In and out of the hospital all his brief life, Peter nevertheless developed into a radiant person who was an inspiration to those fortunate enough to know him. A subtle sense of humor made him a delightful companion, and one had the feeling that every little bit of life was greatly appreciated

by him, most likely because he knew that each day that
came might be his last.

On occasions when infection wracked his lungs and
he gasped for air, he would call to his mother and
whisper, "Say the mantra." Muriel would take his hands
in hers and slowly say these words, breathing deeply
and giving him a chance to breathe as well and as deeply
as he was able:

> Quietness
> Calmness
> God's love
> Our love
> The love of those who love us
> And those whom we love
> Surrounds us now.

In the name of the Father, and of the Son, and of the Holy
Spirit. Amen.

These words, along with the deep breathing, would calm
his choking, and after several times of repeating, he
would breathe more easily and be able to relax.

When I awake in the middle of the night and cannot
again find sleep, I lie quietly. Relaxed and breathing
deeply I also "say the words." I know them now so well
that I do not even have to form the syllables. The
concepts form themselves in my mind and penetrate to
the heart of my consciousness. They do not always bring
sleep, but they calm my troubled mind, and I can rest,
knowing that God is caring for me and underneath are
the everlasting arms.

Many periods of deep breathing daily refill the empty
and depleted parts of my being. Listening to a favorite

recording from one of the great composers—Bach, Chopin, Liszt, Beethoven—restores my calmness in the midst of a busy day. A visit to my garden to prune and dig and poke about among the flowers is a never-ending source of delight and restoration of perspective, a drive along the coastline of the Pacific not far from my home: all are restful experiences and connect me to the Source of my being. Sometimes there is little time for any of these favorite techniques. And my favorite techniques would not necessarily be the same as yours, for each is unique. But, I urge you to find those techniques that serve best to make you receptive rather than aggressive and that give you a wider perspective. Practice them, at least some of them, every day. Get a feeling of the eternality of time and the far reaches of distance into your perspective. If you are troubled and there seems to be no immediate answer, remember, this too shall pass away. Nothing remains forever unchanging, except God. Cultivate the habit of talking over your joys and your anger, your unsolved problems and the things that amuse you, with God, just as you would do with a very dear and close friend sitting in the chair opposite you. And then listen for the answer. This is prayer. And it is the greatest source I know for the release of power within you and me. It is the only real answer I have found to the inner energy crisis from which so many of us suffer.

Turning Inside Out

Love starts when another
Person's needs become
More important than your Own.

This anonymous message left on my desk at the close of one of our stress classes speaks an authentic word about the process of turning inside out.

In the course of my own struggle with emotional and mental illnesses, it was the sudden awareness of what was happening to my husband and my son that made their needs more important than my own. For a long time following, I felt that it did not at all matter if I were completely obliterated in the process so long as they had their needs taken care of. The annals of history are full of tremendous feats of impossible physical prowess performed when there was an emergency, and the needs of others loomed as all-important to the one who cared deeply.

When the Yugoslavian nun Mother Teresa witnessed the suffering of the terminally ill thrown out into the streets of Calcutta to die, her deep consciousness was alerted. Because it was superstitiously regarded that one's dying in the home of another or even in one's ancestral home would bring bad luck, she set about finding an old, unused building in that overcrowded city where she was able to bring the dying ones in off the street and established a hospital for the terminally ill.

When sophisticated, worldly-wise Englishman Malcolm Muggeridge, caustic in his observations on British Broadcasting Company's programs, visited the hospital and met Mother Teresa, his entire life took a new direction. He turned inside out and set about the process of raising funds for that hospital, and now, for many additional hospitals around the world where refugees may find sanctuary in their dying hours.

At the very heart of this process of learning to bend without breaking is, I believe, discovering the meaning of one's life.

The eminent psychiatrist Viktor Frankl bases his concept of Logotherapy on the "will to meaning." He asserts that a person is never *driven* to moral behavior; in each instance he *decides* to behave morally. And in making the decision he finds meaning in life. In Nazi prison camps he proved conclusively to himself and saw it demonstrated by hundreds of other prisoners that one can lose every freedom he or she has had and still live productively, provided personal meaning for life can be found. It can never be found, however, unless something or someone outside yourself captures your attention and becomes all-important, taking the focus off yourself. When Jesus said, "He who seeks to save his life shall lose it; but he who loses his life for my sake and the sake of the gospel, shall find it," he spoke one of the most basic truths in life.

In what ways may we find meaning in our lives? I

cannot say for you, because each life is unique. But, if at some terribly low moment in your life someone has come along and offered you hope and a way out of your trouble—and then, if that person or the persons in that group have stood by to help every time you have faltered and become depressed, returning again and again to assure you of their love and support—you know what it's all about. You are turned on again, turned inside out in fact, and your thoughts are no longer morbidly withdrawn but focused outward toward the ones you love and who need your help. You feel joy surging from the depths of your being. You want to run and shout and say "thank you!" And usually you will want to say "thank you, God," for it is incredible that this change could have come about in any other way except by God's extravagant grace that blesses both the just and the unjust. This experience marks for you the change from one sort of life to another.

Have you ever done something of which you were not at all proud, something that was cruel and hurtful toward another, and had the experience of having that person's forgiveness? Have you felt the bond of a restored relationship when you thought it was too badly torn to ever be pieced together? Have you found yourself turning against someone you had previously loved deeply but who became estranged from you because of misunderstanding or unexpressed anger, and then, the barrier of dislike between that person and you was swept aside, and you felt that you at last understood each other, and the love relationship was restored?

This turning inside out has been a very vital part of the Christian faith ever since its beginning. But in some centuries the witness grows dim and the experience demanding that witness ineffective. Alcoholics Anonymous tells its members, "If you have been helped to find a spiritual experience and sobriety through our program, you must be willing to be on call, day or night, to help another."

So it is with stress techniques, I strongly feel. You have learned why you respond as you do when you are deeply depressed or anxious and are undergoing a period of overstress. And you have taken the first steps. As a result, if you have been helped to handle your emotional problems, and both your self-esteem and your perspective have been restored, is it not also incumbent upon you to look about you and find someone who needs your help? This is the only way I know whereby the experience of being helped and of finding new meaning for your life can be fed and kept alive.

Look about you to discover the spontaneously happy persons. They are the ones who give away the most. They never seem to have much need for attention. They have got themselves off their hands! They're into a dozen interesting things; and yet they seem always to have time to sit down and listen to another's problems.

A woman in my close acquaintance is just such a person. Although she works at a rather menial job to augment the family income, she still finds time to take care of her home and her husband; and on one of her two days off in a week, she takes care also of her two grandchildren. She has had several bouts with surgery and is gradually losing her hearing, but she never allows herself to be anxious about the outcome. She is greatly beloved by a circle of friends in her church and at work and will do a favor for anyone who needs her help. She seldom asks for a favor for herself. She will never be listed as one of the world's great people, because her circle of living is limited. But she is one of the most loving, giving persons I know—and one of the happiest. She truly knows all about turning inside out.

Another friend, whose life ended tragically, could not possibly go through the turning-inside-out process because she did not have enough self-esteem to guarantee her safety in that "outside world." One of the most brilliant persons I have ever known was also one of the most creative. A Phi Beta Kappa graduate of a western university, she started writing children's stories. And although she was too timid to show them to her friends, a counselor friend to whom she had shown them told me they were exquisitely well done and deserving of special publication. Her childhood had been made miserable by a sibling rivalry with a sister whom her mother loved far more than she did my friend. Her marriage was unfortunate and to a man of a different religious faith. Eventually she drifted away from the church but could not find sufficient anchor for support. In a fit of despondency she took her own life.

I relate this story to illustrate the fact that it is impossible to turn inside out until certain preliminary steps are taken. There had never been any ego buildup in her growing-up years. And I suppose in a life such as hers, unless outside factors were favorable, it would be impossible to gain enough self-esteem even from a small group of friends. Perhaps this is why Alcoholics Anonymous makes its turning inside out the last step.

At the heart of this experience of learning to bend without breaking, then, is the absolute necessity of finding meaning for your life. You don't find it by frontal attack but by forgetting yourself. But in order to go through this process, you must know who is in control.

Through a long, slow process I am learning that trying to manipulate people is detrimental to them as well as to self. The more insecure you are, the greater the need to hold the reins in your own hands and exercise that control. There is a yearning for order out of chaos and for a safe environment. In my better moments I have learned that it is usually best not to get into the middle of the mess and try either to stir things up or insist upon putting them to rights. The better way for the one with the nervous temperament is to allow God to do the stirring while you wait for his direction toward change.

Too many of us have regarded a commitment to religious faith as the drawing up of some sort of contract with the Most High. "I'll do this for you, God, if you'll do certain things for me" is really what we mean when we say, "Lord, I want to be a Christian." It's like hiring God to shore us up in carrying out our own details. "Today, God, help me to do my good deed, help me keep calm and poised so the big deal I'm putting across will go successfully, help me to win friends and influence people. You see to it that my daughter loves me and quits disliking me for my thoughtlessness of her mother and my insensitivity in handling her; help my wife to keep on being the peacemaker of the family, because I, dear God, just don't have the time to see to all the details involved. You, please, speak to Mr. X who walked out of my staff meeting the other day, and help him see my viewpoint."

But, suppose God is trying to say to us, "Remember, I am President, and you are the administrative assistant. If you will become teachable and listen, I'll tell you what I think ought to be done. Remember, my perspective is different from yours. I'll give you hints and ideas from time to time, but I will seldom map out the plan in detail. I expect you to be my representative; and because I am not seen in the way in which people see one another, you'll have to be my voice, my hands, my feet, my touch. When people talk to you and listen, I want them to get a strong idea of who I am and what I am like."

I am very certain that if I had not early turned my life over to God as my final authority and controlling force, I'd have broken beyond repair. There is no other way in which I could have handled the load of overstress! Painfully I am learning, over and over again, to resign that self-propelled struggle and allow God to dictate the terms. And I have to keep relearning; for such resignation restores the balance between will power and relaxation. The philosopher William James is reported to have said, "Religion is the relaxation of the effort to be self-sufficient." It is, I think, getting yourself off your hands so you are free to reach out your hands to the world.

This is the essence of Christianity, is it not? You begin with a belief that there is a Power greater than your own, and you turn your life over to that Power. Different persons conceive of God in different ways, but to me that Power is my Father, God, very much as Jesus thought him to be. When I remember this frame of reference and my commitment, I am secure, even though my body symptoms may not always indicate the same. But I, the essential being that I am, find a sense of security in that knowledge and commitment. It isn't just a feeling. It's believing when you cannot prove. It is believing that he is there whether I can sense his presence or not. I am captive of that commitment and to that Presence. In the course of the quest I have learned much about where my own self-worth lies, and I am sometimes able to endorse myself, especially because I have never quite given up the search and the commitment. Then, in gratitude for life and what God has done for me, I keep trying to look outward as much as possible to the needs of those about me. As a result, I find myself "turning inside out" in order to try to help others as I have been helped. The process may sound simple, but it is the greatest and most difficult metamorphosis and re-creation in the world!

Beyond committing yourself to a Power greater than your own, it is very necessary to have a support system. My basic religious faith has been my mainstay throughout my life. I grew up being loved. I have the support of a wonderful husband and a thoughtful son. Each year I realize that a host of friends support me and love me also. Without such support, I doubt I could have made it. I am humbled and deeply grateful to God for these gifts.

Because so many people deeply troubled find their support systems swept away, they find, alas, that they cannot stand alone. This is the reason I am deeply concerned that churches provide support groups for the troubled ones.

One further thing I must constantly tell myself is that the victim of a psychoneurosis, just as the victim of alcoholism, may never be quite sure how much more bending with overloads of stress he or she can take without breaking. This is to say the problem is arrested but not completely cured. Realizing this fact makes one humble, indeed, and in need of constantly practicing the will techniques as well as the relaxation and meditation techniques. And it means continuing to turn over the controls to a Power greater than your own.

This is the end of my story, but its writing is a dream fulfilled. Because of its very personal nature, it has not been easy to make myself vulnerable. And much of it has been written during a period of outer stress. If I am to be of help to others who struggle with problems akin to mine, I must be willing to be vulnerable. For better or for worse, it is my thank-you letter to God who was always there when I seemed to be up against a blank wall with no way out. And he is still there!

Praise God from whom all blessings flow!

Appendix A

"How Much Change Can You Take?"

Dr. Thomas Holmes, professor of psychiatry at the University of Washington, has devised a scale assigning point value to changes, good and bad, that often affect us. When enough changes occur during one year to add up to 300, a danger point has been reached. In the population he studied, 80 percent of the people who exceeded 300 became seriously depressed, had heart attacks, or suffered other serious illness. The following is an adaptation.

Life Change	Points
Death of spouse	100
Divorce	73
Marital separation	65
Jail term	63
Death of close family member	63
Personal injury or illness	53
Marriage	50
Fired at work	47
Marital reconciliation	45
Retirement	45
Change in health of family member	44
Pregnancy	40
Sex difficulties	39
Gain of new family member	39
Change in financial state	38
Death of close friend	37
Change to different line of work	36

Change in number of arguments with spouse 35
Foreclosure of mortgage or loan 30
Change in responsibilities at work 29
Son or daughter leaving home 29
Trouble with in-laws 29
Outstanding personal achievement 28
Wife begin or stop work 26
Begin or end school 26
Revision of personal habits 24
Trouble with boss 23
Change in residence 20
Change in schools 20
Vacation 13
Minor violations of the law 11

Instruction for Use of Stress Chart

In the stress classes I have taught in various churches, I have handed 3″ X 5″ cards to class members, asking them to do three things:

a) Using the stress chart as it now appears in the appendix, I have asked them to score themselves for one year—the past one—listing on another paper the stresses that appear on the chart and adding the score. This they are to tabulate on the card.

b) Using any twelve-month period during the course of their life, count the number of stresses, and assess the score that appears on the chart. This, of course, will have been their "most stressful year." Under b on the card, write the score.

c) Turning the card over to the other side, number from one to five, and list the five greatest stresses at the present time, in order of their intensity. We find many varying stresses not suggested on the Holmes stress chart that are as real and as distressing, such as change in life-style on the part of a family member, or radical changes in the character or life-styles of members of the neighborhood where I live, or the present drug problem on the part of someone I love.

A week is given to complete the assignment and no name is to be attached to the card. But cards are to be tabulated and handed in at the second session, after there is plenty of time for consideration on the part of each member. Scores are posted on a blackboard for all to see, but the anonymity of those participating is protected. It is helpful for the leader of the class to learn of the average stress score and some of the stresses troubling members of the group.

Appendix B

The Twelve Steps of Alcoholics Anonymous

Step One
   "We admitted we were powerless over alcohol—that our lives had become unmanageable."
Step Two
   "Came to believe that a Power greater than ourselves could restore us to sanity."
Step Three
   "Made a decision to turn our will and our lives over to the care of God as we understood Him."
Step Four
   "Made a searching and fearless moral inventory of ourselves."
Step Five
   "Admitted to God, to ourselves, and to another human being, the exact nature of our wrongs."
Step Six
   "Were entirely ready to have God remove all these defects of character."
Step Seven
   "Humbly asked Him to remove our shortcomings."
Step Eight
   "Made a list of all persons we had harmed, and became willing to make amends to them all."
Step Nine
   "Made direct amends to such people wherever possible, except when to do so would injure them or others."
Step Ten
   "Continued to make personal inventory and when we were wrong promptly admitted it."
Step Eleven
   "Sought through prayer and meditation to improve our conscious contact with God as we understood Him, praying only for knowledge of His will for us and the power to carry that out."
Step Twelve
   "Having had a spiritual awakening as the result of these steps, we tried to carry this message to alcoholics, and to practice these principles in all our affairs."

Appendix C

A Suggested Plan for Discussion in Church Stress Groups

1. Begin with a brief period of relaxation, quiet, prayer.
2. Each week discuss one chapter of the book. Members may take turns introducing the chapter and starting the discussion. If members want to continue meeting after the chapters of the book *To Bend Without Breaking* are concluded, they may wish to choose additional resources and share them in subsequent weeks.
3. Each week select a few members of the group (depending on the size of the group and the time available) to share minor incidents of stress that have happened recently. (For example: "On Tuesday I baked and decorated a cake for my husband's birthday party. When I came home from work, I found my son had cut a piece right out of it!") It is important that the incident be a relatively minor problem. By getting at the reaction and solution to this kind of problem, you grow a step closer to dealing with truly major ones.

   Discussion participants chosen for the meeting should prepare illustrations carefully before the meeting. A timekeeper should be selected who will start discussion and notify each person when his or her time is up. (The group should set, by consensus, the maximum time to be allowed each person for the presentation.)

   In the discussion, follow this outline:

   a) *Describe the stressful situation carefully.* Time? Place? Persons involved?

b) *Describe the way your body responded.* Did the stress seem to be located in particular places? Where?
c) *Discuss your emotional reaction.* Anger? Embarrassment? How did you feel about it?
d) *What did you do about the stressful incident?* (For instance: "I blew up and gave him a piece of my mind," or "I decided to keep still because I dreaded a real confrontation.") Be honest. Don't try to justify or judge negatively what you did. Just describe the reaction.
e) *Did your Christian faith make any difference in the way you handled the situation?* If not, say so. Don't try to put on something that did not happen. Discussion can turn phony and artificial here if there is not complete honesty and an atmosphere of real acceptance in the group.
f) *What difference might your Christian faith make in the future that it didn't make in the situation you have described?*

4. Ask members of the group to react, without judging or giving advice. Perhaps they have been in similar situations and would like to share the way in which they handled the problem. If they think the person who gave the incident handled it well, they should make it known to the group that they think it was handled well. Perhaps the incident is not closed, and the person to which it happened is still mulling it over. In this case suggestions may be very helpful. Do not criticize. Be as objective as possible and as loving in offering possible solutions.

5. Close the meeting with another brief period of quiet and with prayer. Several may participate, or, if the group prefers, one may lead in prayer at each meeting. As the group develops, considerable flexibility may occur here as well as at the start of the sharing session.

Recovery –

Exercise –
   Swimming
   brisk walking

<u>The</u> <u>Little</u> <u>Locksmith</u>

   Deal with panic of fear
 · Prayer –

      Heart of medicine
   is contingency – to God –

Relaxation techniques

   Timshell – Thou mayest

East of Eden – Steinbeck
      receptivity